Managing Change in the Workplace

Managing Change in the Workplace

SHEILA J. COSTELLO

Business Skills Express Series

IRWIN
Professional Publishing

MIRROR PRESS

Burr Ridge, Illinois
New York, New York
Boston, Massachusetts

IRWIN
Concerned About Our Environment

In recognition of the fact that our company is a large end-user of fragile yet replenishable resources, we at IRWIN can assure you that every effort is made to meet or exceed Environmental Protection Agency (EPA) recommendations and requirements for a "greener" workplace.

To preserve these natural assets, a number of environmental policies, both companywide and department-specific, have been implemented. From the use of 50% recycled paper in our textbooks to the printing of promotional materials with recycled stock and soy inks to our office paper recycling program, we are committed to reducing waste and replacing environmentally unsafe products with safer alternatives.

Mirror Press:	David R. Helmstadter
	Carla F. Tishler
Editor-in-chief:	Jeffrey A. Krames
Project editor:	Amy E. Lund
Production manager:	Bob Lange
Interior designer:	Jeanne M. Rivera
Cover designer:	Tim Kaage
Art manager:	Kim Meriwether
Art studio:	Electra Graphics, Inc.
Compositor:	Alexander Typesetting, Inc.
Typeface:	12/14 Criterion
Printer:	Malloy Lithographing, Inc.

Library of Congress Cataloging-in-Publication Data

Costello, Sheila J.
  Managing change in the workplace / Sheila J. Costello.
      p.   cm. — (Business skills express series)
    ISBN 0-7863-0162-7
      1. Organizational change—Management.   I. Title.   II. Series:
  Business skills express.
    HD58.8.C67   1994
    658.4′063—dc20   93–40306

Printed in the United States of America
1 2 3 4 5 6 7 8 9 0 ML 0 1 9 8 7 6 5 4

PREFACE

Change is a natural and inevitable part of organizational life. Whether driven by reactions to external market demands or internal desires for continuous improvement, change is a constant. Far less constant, however, is how well we understand and manage it.

This book provides you with a rich understanding of the change process—its impact on you and the people you work with. It provides practical guidance and job-related exercises for planning and managing change, enabling you to facilitate positive rather than negative change experiences within your organization. Critical and timely change management questions are addressed in a step-by-step approach. Key discussions are designed to help you better understand and facilitate the overall change process. Filled with many examples and case studies, this book will enable you to learn from the mistakes as well as the successes of others.

Sheila J. Costello

ABOUT THE AUTHOR

Sheila J. Costello, Principal of SJC Associates, Beverly, MA, is a private consultant specializing in management training and development. With over 18 years of professional training and management experience, she has provided services to a wide variety of private and public organizations, including several Fortune 500 companies.

Ms. Costello has also held positions as national Director of Training and Development for American Mutual Insurance Companies, Manager of Training for AtlantiCare Medical Center and Corporations, Regional Program Director for International Training Corporation, Director for the Center for Business and Industry at Massachusetts Bay Community College, Program Director for the Bentley College Center for Continuing and Professional Education, and Parent Involvement Unit Coordinator for all of Boston's Head Start Programs. She continues to serve as an adjunct faculty member for several private and public colleges and associations, training business professionals in a variety of management skills. Having spent many years as a manager, she is committed to providing practical rather than theoretical information to address many of today's management concerns.

ABOUT IRWIN PROFESSIONAL PUBLISHING

Irwin Professional Publishing is the nation's premier publisher of business books. As a Times Mirror company, we work closely with Times Mirror training organizations, including Zenger-Miller, Inc., Learning International, Inc., and Kaset International, to serve the training needs of business and industry.

About the Business Skills Express Series

This expanding series of authoritative, concise, and fast-paced books delivers high-quality training on key business topics at a remarkably affordable cost. The series will help managers, supervisors, and frontline personnel in organizations of all sizes and types hone their business skills while enhancing job performance and career satisfaction.

Business Skills Express books are ideal for employee seminars, independent self-study, on-the-job training, and classroom-based instruction. Express books are also convenient-to-use references at work.

CONTENTS

Self-Assessment

As a way of assessing how much you already know and are using in your day-to-day management of change, complete this simple pretest. It may confirm your confidence in your knowledge and ability for managing change, or it may raise some useful questions that will start you on your quest of learning how to manage change more effectively. In either case, it will provide you with a starting point as you explore this book.

Read each statement carefully and place a check (✓) on the appropriate line to indicate your level of agreement or disagreement.

	Almost Always	Sometimes	Almost Never
1. Organizations would be better off if they followed the motto "If it's not broken, why fix it?"			✓
2. Managing change begins by focusing first on people who have to carry it out.			✓
3. When new ideas don't fit existing organizational rules and regulations, they should either be screened out or altered until they do fit.		✓	
4. When organizational change is announced, the first thing people want to know is how it will affect the organization.			✓
5. All major changes are equally difficult to manage.			✓
6. The best way to introduce change is quickly and decisively.			✓
7. Change occurs as long as the person at the top wants it.			✓
8. The only cost in failing to manage change effectively is that the change doesn't occur.		✓	
9. People usually resist a change because they don't like it.	✓		
10. As long as people are made aware of a change, they will accept it.		✓	

If you did not check "almost never" for every statement, you have much to learn about organizational change. The content of each statement is addressed in its corresponding chapter number. For example, Chapter 1 addresses statement 1, Chapter 2 addresses statement 2, and so on. By the time you have completed this book, you will know why "almost never" is the correct response for all 10 statements.

1 | Choosing to Change

This chapter will help you to:

- Understand the past and present organizational context for change.
- Define change.
- Identify what causes change.

Making Choices

The Doright Corporation was founded in 1950 on the east coast by two engineers, Mark Paulson and Wendy Peterson. They had developed and patented a technique for building a special engine component for aircraft carrier manufacturers. Their name, Doright, reflected their corporate philosophy to a "T." While their product development processes were laborious and expensive, their work was meticulous, and their customers were very satisfied.

Between 1950 and 1970, the company experienced tremendous growth and could boast that they had cornered the market with their product. They attributed much of their success to their original design and manufacturing techniques, which they had adhered to consistently over the previous 20 years. With a captive market and no outside competition, their techniques had gone virtually unchanged.

As the company entered the 1970s, the business climate of the aircraft industry began to shift. More and more regulations were placed on the aircraft industry, while others were lifted. Concerns grew over production costs and speed. Increasing product competition emerged from the west coast and Europe. New designs were

1

developed and tested successfully by other manufacturers on a monthly basis. New manufacturing techniques were adopted regularly as new technologies advanced.

In response to these escalating pressures, Doright dug its heels in. It launched a huge marketing campaign using slogans such as "If it's not broken, why fix it? Stay with the company that has been doing it right for 20 years. Buy Doright. You know it will be right." Unfortunately, in spite of valiant efforts, Doright experienced spiraling downturns in market share and five years later declared Chapter 11 bankruptcy. ■

Questions to Consider

1. What went wrong for the Doright Corporation?

> They did nothing to advance themselves
> in technology or

2. If you had managed the Doright Corporation, what, if anything, would you have done differently to prevent its demise?

3. If you managed the Doright Corporation after the announcement of Chapter 11 bankruptcy, what suggestions would you make for turning the company around?

4. What happens to companies that live too long with the motto "If it's not broken, why fix it"?

ORGANIZATIONAL CONTEXT FOR CHANGE

1

Historically, many organizations have managed in the same way that the Doright Corporation managed. Mottos such as "If it's not broken, why fix it?" were commonly heard and, in many cases, were woven into the fabric of organizational culture. Unfortunately, stagnation and self-destruction often followed, causing organizations to experience much the same fate as Doright.

Still other organizations began to adopt the philosophy that speed was the answer, and if they could only make things faster, they would take the market by storm. Speed did produce things faster, but, unfortunately, quality was not always controlled. As a result, the cost of rework or lost customers due to poor quality often met or exceeded any savings acquired through the speed of production.

Today, organizations and companies throughout the world are embracing revolutionary methods of working. They are focusing not only on efficiency, but on quality. Organizations that want to stay competitive and respond to increasing customer demands are developing and incorporating new views about change. Change is no longer a forced response to external pressures or major internal problems that have been unattended to for too long and now must be fixed to prevent disaster. Change is a natural and encouraged process, embraced as a means to continually improve and renew organizational vitality. Healthy organizations choose to change as a way of staying competitive; they seldom wait until they are forced.

Change is by no means a new concept, yet it is occurring at a faster pace and with greater complexity than ever before. Change is everywhere. We all face growing responsibilities for not only managing, but initiating needed changes to keep our organizations moving forward. As a result, managers must understand and manage change well to succeed. It is no longer a "nice-to-know" skill; managing change is an essential skill called upon daily in organizations everywhere.

Here are some of the changes organizations face today:

- Computerization for business and production.
- Mergers, expansions, acquisitions, insolvencies, buyouts, and Chapter 11 bankruptcies.
- Reorganizations and restructurings.
- New approaches to improving competitiveness: total quality management, continuous improvement, and integrated work teams.
- Technological advances that shift work methodologies.
- Increased customer demands and focus.
- Increased opportunities and competition caused by a growing global marketplace and trade agreement shifts.
- New product and market development.
- Compliance with new regulations from local government agencies to the International Standards Organization (ISO).
- Greater diversity in the workforce: age, race, culture, gender, education, language, and so on.
- Economic fluctuations affecting business decisions.
- Organizational cultures redefined to meet growing demands of the world around us.

■ Exercise 1.1

List the changes you have observed in your own organization over the past year.

_____

_____

_____

_____

_____

WHAT IS CHANGE?

Change is "the act, process, or result of changing: as alteration, transformation, or substitution" (*Webster's Tenth New Collegiate Dictionary*, 1993).

In the Chinese culture, change is viewed somewhat differently. It is customary to see change characterized by the following symbols.

危 — Potential dangers　　　　機 — Hidden opportunities

Change is viewed as something with both hidden opportunities and potential dangers. In the chapter opening vignette, Doright's hidden opportunities may have been to continually improve to stay on top. The potential dangers, which were later realized, were the negative ramifications of maintaining the status quo or not changing.

In Greece, the letter delta (a triangle) is used to symbolize change. Strangely enough, the triangle is also the most stable geometric form. Through change there can also be stability. Again, if Doright had changed to keep up with the times it may have remained a stable company.

WHAT CAUSES CHANGE?

Change can be caused by a response to either existing or anticipated pain as well as by the mere desire to continually improve. Often these factors exist simultaneously, but the presence of any one of them alone can serve as a catalyst for change.

Some companies are forced to change when they can no longer exist maintaining the status quo. Changes of this nature are generally reactive and can be highly traumatic for organizations. Other companies choose to change in an effort to improve. Their changes generally are proactive and often more developmental in nature.

As organizations work to continually improve themselves, they are less likely to experience major transformational changes. For this reason, the changes tend to be easier to manage and have fewer long-term, devastating effects on organizations.

The chart on page 6 depicts the reactive and proactive components of change. Far too often, change does not occur until the current pain reaches an extremely high level, and organizations are forced to react for survival purposes. Often too much change is needed at too fast a pace for organizations to survive it. Even if short-term survival is accomplished using this approach, major casualties and scarring often result.

	Danger	Opportunity
Anticipated Pain (What's expected)	**Situation**: Product competition may increase; customers may demand higher quality and lower costs in the future. **Pain of maintaining status quo**: Potential loss of market share, company survival, job security, etc.	**Situation**: Future planning; repositioning to endure and profit from what is expected to happen. **Pain of maintaining status quo**: Loss of a gain that was possible to achieve (e.g. maintain or increase market share). <div align="center">**Proactive**</div>
Current Pain (What's happening now?)	**Situation**: Product competition has increased; customers are demanding higher quality and lower costs. **Pain of maintaining status quo**: Immediate loss of market share, job security, growing threat to company survival, etc.	**Situation**: Take care of this situation with immediate action and restore competitive edge. **Pain of maintaining status quo**: Loss of a gain that is within grasp (e.g. maintain or increase market share). <div align="center">**Reactive**</div>

Source: Adapted from *Managing Organizational Change: Implementation Planning Procedure,* p. 14, Copyright 1990, with permission of Daryl R. Conner, ODR, Inc., 2900 Chamblee–Tucker Rd., Atlanta, GA 30341.

Organizations that have the foresight to anticipate needed changes before disaster strikes are in better shape. This proactive approach reduces the need to engage in firefighting techniques. It can allow a company to plan and implement change much more effectively.

In either case, pain, whether antiticpated or current, can drive change. Maintaining the status quo no longer becomes an acceptable option for conducting business.

Exercise 1.2

Consider a problem situation in your organization that you believe may be driving a particular change. First, fill in the boxes in the following chart based on anticipated pain, and then project current pain should the status quo be maintained. You may want to begin brainstorming possible solutions to these situations.

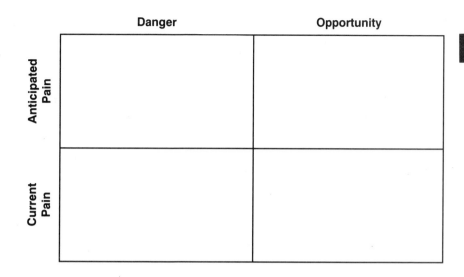

As you foster and manage change by encouraging people to be proactive rather than reactive, you may want to consider engaging them in an activity similar to Exercise 1.2. As situations are mapped out, it becomes easier to see how much more effective you can be by anticipating pain and responding to it in a timely manner.

CHANGE DRIVEN BY CHOICE

Many market-conscious organizations are *choosing* to change. They incorporate change as natural, inevitable, and healthy. Even if pain is an underlying motivator, some organizations are committed to improving themselves continually. They are driven more by the contagiousness of success than by a fear of failure.

■ E x e r c i s e   1 . 3

Describe a situation or area in your work that you feel is going well. Brainstorm possible ways you might further improve upon it to add value.

1

Situation or Area:

_____

_____

_____

_____

_____

Possible Improvements:

_____

_____

_____

_____

_____

Chapter 1 Checkpoints

✓ Organizations that adopt an "If it's not broken, why fix it?" philosophy tend to maintain the status quo too long and lose out on vital opportunities to keep themselves competitive and healthy.

✓ Change is occurring at a faster pace and with greater complexity than ever before.

✓ Change is the act, process, or result of changing and includes alteration, transformation, and substitution.

✓ Change can be caused by a response to anticipated or existing pain as well as by the desire to continually improve.

2 Change Begins from Within

This chapter will help you to:

- Increase awareness of your own feelings about and reactions to change.
- Define the term *frame of reference*.
- Learn how frames of reference influence your reactions to change.

Great Expectations #1

Juanita Martinez is the office manager for the Registry of Motor Vehicles. Due to a recent consolidation and increased workload, she needed to change several job assignments as well as the physical layout of several work areas. After giving it some thought, she decided to tackle the physical changes first. She sensed she would have few to no objections to these changes, and at least she would start things off on a positive note.

Her first change affected her own secretary, Kim Hwong, who had been at the same workstation for the past eight years. Because Juanita was moving her own office across the hall, she wanted Kim to relocate to an area just outside of it. The new space was similar to Kim's present space, and she would have the same resources. Juanita thought Kim would readily accept this change. In fact, she believed Kim would be thrilled with it because the new space had a window.

Juanita called Kim into her office to inform her about the new space plans. She could see by the look on Kim's face that she was not at all happy with this change. Juanita asked Kim if she wanted to talk about it, and Kim replied, "No, it's okay." The meeting was concluded at that point, and Kim went back to work. Her production was slower than usual, and she seemed sad most of the day. ■

■ Questions to Consider

1. What went wrong?

_____

_____

_____

2. If you were Juanita, how might you have managed this situation differently?

_____

_____

_____

3. What could you do to support Kim in the change process now?

_____

_____

_____

Great Expectations #2

Months passed and the physical changes were finalized. Juanita was now ready to make job assignment changes. She needed to combine two jobs—initial intake and photography—into one. Fortunately, she had lost her photographer through attrition, and so the natural candidate for the combination job was Mark Myers, the initial intake worker.

She called him into her office and explained the new plan. Mark was thrilled by the idea and said, "That's great. I've always wanted to try that job too. Most of the time there's a delay between customers, so I think I'll be able to fit it in pretty easily. The morning will probably be our busiest time, so I'll have to think about how we can streamline our process. I think this might even be fun. I've always wanted to learn how to operate our camera, and I've been getting a little bored with just doing the intakes."

Before concluding the meeting, Juanita asked Mark if he had any questions. He responded, "When do we get started?" Juanita replied, "How about next week?"

Mark smiled as he replied, "Fine." Mark left the office. He appeared highly productive and happy all day. ■

■ Questions to Consider

1. How do you feel the beginning of this change effort went?

_____

_____

_____

2. What do you think accounts for the difference between Kim's and Mark's change reactions?

_____

_____

_____

3. How do these two vignettes relate to your own work situations, and what are the implications for management?

_____

_____

_____

HOW DO YOU REACT TO CHANGE?

As you've seen from the chapter opening vignettes, there may be great differences in how people react to change. As a leader of change, you must realize that change begins with the individual and is based on individual experiences, education, background, and so on. In order for you to lead change effectively, you should understand your own feelings about and reactions to change. Looking inward is an important first step before exploring ways to help others cope with change.

■ Exercise 2.1

Often just the word *change* conjures up many feelings. Think about the word and your experiences with it. List your reactions, thoughts, feelings, values, notions, abilities, and beliefs about change. Focus on a specific change if it helps.

My Own Feelings and Reactions to Change:

_____

_____

_____

_____

_____

Compare your list with others' lists. While some people view change as a very positive event, others may feel extremely negative about it. Still others may experience a combination of the two reactions, which may be greatly influenced by the type of change, how it affects them, and how it is managed. Take a look once again at your own responses and try to determine which way the scales tip for you.

Listed below are some typical responses to this exercise.

Feelings about Change	
(+) Positive	(−) Negative
Exciting	Frustrating
Challenging	Fear of unknown
Growth opportunity	Pessimism: "It'll never work"
New skills	Fear of failure
Job enrichment	More work
Diversity	Change in routine
Increased job security	Decreased job security
Involvement	Poor communication

You may have noticed that there can be a positive side to every negative, just as there is opportunity in the face of danger (as discussed in Chapter 1).

■ Exercise 2.2

How do you believe your employees would respond to Exercise 2.1?

_____

_____

_____

_____

_____

2

While your employees' responses may or may not be similar to yours, you will find that they will reflect many of the typical responses listed on page 14. This will be true regardless of whether or not they have management responsibilities. Far too often, managers believe that employees will somehow react differently to change than managers do, yet this is seldom the case. On occasion, however, you may discover a little more negativity on the part of employees, but not because they are so different from managers. Rather, employees may react differently to change because they may have been treated differently in the change process. Increased negative feelings may reflect lack of awareness, understanding, or acceptance of a change, often arising from poor communication or lack of involvement.

Keep in mind that individual employees, even in the same change situation, may not share viewpoints. You will discover a wide variety of responses to change, ranging from the person who is totally traumatized by moving a desk a half inch to the person who, in the face of total reorganization, says, "Great! Give me more."

Your job is to be aware of yourself and your influence on others as well as to be able to understand and respond to the individual change reactions of those you manage.

WHAT IS A FRAME OF REFERENCE?

Where do the differing feelings about and reactions to change come from? Generally, they are determined by the individual's frame of reference. A frame of reference is a filter for viewing and reacting to the world around you. Formed and shaped by your background and experiences, it is influenced by many facets of your life, including education, race, gender, culture, place of birth, development, parents, friends, associates, personality, and values. Given human diversity, frames of reference vary greatly from one person to another.

HOW DO FRAMES OF REFERENCE INFLUENCE YOUR REACTIONS TO CHANGE?

Your frame of reference can greatly influence what you perceive, process, think, decide, believe, and expect about change. It acts as a filter that determines your actions and reactions.

Information is received and processed through our frame-of-reference filters, influencing the following:

- Perceptions.
- Ideas and thoughts.
- Beliefs and expectations.
- Decision-making processes.
- Critical thinking processes.

These factors influence one another and lead to *action*. Thus, a particular frame of reference will lead to particular actions and reactions. This phenomenon explains why there is often such diversity in reaction to a change experience.

Examples to Consider

Here are some typical examples of frame-of-reference influences:

Example 1:   It is close to the holidays and raining outside. A child, looking out of the window and observing the rain, turns to his mother and asks, "Mommy, does this mean that Santa's reindeers are coming?" The child obviously perceives a relationship between rain and *rein*deer.

Example 2:   At the sound of a ringing telephone a father says to his child, "Don't worry, the answering machine will pick it up." The child responds, "But Daddy, the answering machine doesn't have any hands." In this case, the concept of how answering machines work is not a part of the child's frame of reference.

Example 3:   Three American managers are sent to negotiate a business deal with the president of a Thai corporation. At the start of the meeting, the Americans demonstrate what they felt would be customary courtesy by extending a handshake. By the close of the meeting, the deal was off. The Thai president had been insulted, because in Thailand it is customary to bow your head lower than the individual to whom you wish to show respect.

■ Exercise 2.3

Select an employee who has difficulties regarding change, due perhaps to misunderstandings or disagreements. Make a detailed list of the person's likes, dislikes, background, abilities, and so on until you have a fairly good idea of his frame of reference. Be sure to include information regarding the employee's past history with change—positive or negative. Next, make a similar list for yourself. Compare the two lists to determine frame of reference differences that could account for the misunderstandings or disagreements.

Frame of Reference	
My Employee's	**Mine**
_____	_____
_____	_____
_____	_____
_____	_____
_____	_____
_____	_____
_____	_____
_____	_____

1. What differences might account for the difficulties?

_____

_____

_____

_____

_____

2. What ideas do you have for resolving these differences?

_____

_____

_____

_____

_____

Exploring the concept of frames of reference will help you better understand and work with people in the change process. As you communicate with people about change, try to put your messages into the receiver's frame of reference. If you are receiving communication regarding a change, try to decipher what you hear by considering the sender's frame of reference. Remember, the only message that counts is the one that is received. Phrase messages in ways that receivers will hear and understand.

Chapter 2 Checkpoints

✓ Managing change begins with the individual. To lead change effectively, you must start by examining your own feelings about and
reactions to change.

✓ A frame of reference is a compilation of your background and experience that serves as a filter for viewing and reacting to the world
around you.

✓ Frames of reference can greatly affect your reactions to change by
influencing what you perceive, process, think, decide, believe, and
expect about change.

3 | Paradigms: Paralysis or Opportunity?

This chapter will help you to:

- Define paradigms.
- Understand how and why paradigms affect change.
- Overcome paradigm paralysis.

Paradigm Perils

It was 10:00 AM and Linda Levitz, software development manager of CompuMed, had called a departmental planning meeting. Her charge was to lead her group in the development of some new health care delivery tracking software called HealthTrac. Driven by an escalating need for health care providers to respond to a multitude of changes in health care delivery systems, HealthTrac was an important and timely project. If successful, this product would be the first of its kind and would be highly marketable.

Linda opened the meeting: "The purpose of our meeting today is to try to visualize what our new product, HealthTrac, will look like. Perhaps the best way of getting started is to go around the room brainstorming ideas." She turned to her right and said, "Let's get started with Tim." Tim shrugged his shoulders and said, "I don't have a clue."

As the discussion moved around the room, the frozen silence began to break, and various ideas were offered. Unfortunately, many of them had remarkable resemblance to software applications they had developed in the past. Other employees simply said, "Pass," as a way of expressing that they had no new ideas to share.

3

Suddenly Jared, a new recruit, offered what Linda thought was an extremely innovative idea. Resounding responses were heard from the floor, including messages such as "That'll never work." "We can't possibly do that!" "No way!" "You've got to be kidding!" "We don't do it that way here."

Jared sank back in his chair and had little to say for the rest of the meeting. Linda continued the meeting for another half hour, and, for the most part, no new concepts were generated. Before closing the meeting, she summarized the group's ideas. As the managers filed out one by one, Linda sat in quiet resignation, thinking to herself how very little had been accomplished and wondering how she might move this group forward. ■

Questions to Consider

1. What went wrong with the brainstorming meeting?

_____

_____

_____

2. If you were the manager, how would you have handled this situation differently?

_____

_____

_____

3. What are some of the implications for Linda, her department, and the company if the new product is not developed successfully?

_____

_____

_____

WHAT ARE PARADIGMS?

As they relate to organizations, *paradigms* are sets of rules and regulations that establish boundaries for making day-to-day business decisions. Because they are often formulated on the basis of past success, they are often referred to as road maps for achieving future success. In the chapter opening vignette, CompuMed employees had great difficulty visualizing the new product, HealthTrac, and most of their suggestions were limited by past experience. The paradigm may well have been that software products needed to look and be developed in a certain way that was familiar to them.

Other examples of typical organizational paradigms include the following:

- Top-down management principles.
- Scientific method applied to problem solving.
- Departmentalization of organizations.
- Clear differentiation of job assignments.

As you review this list, you may think to yourself that some of these paradigms have already changed in organizations you've known. This may be true and will be explained in further detail throughout this chapter.

■ Exercise 3.1

List some paradigms that you believe exist in your own organization today.

_____

_____

_____

_____

_____

CAN PARADIGMS AFFECT CHANGE?

Much like frames of reference, paradigms can become filters that screen information and influence decisions. Problems can occur when incoming information does not fit the existing paradigms. People tend to either screen out information or change it until it does fit. Remember the response to Jared's new ideas in the chapter opening vignette? Try to imagine, for instance:

- A square wheel.
- A purple orange.
- A two-wheeled car.

It seems almost incomprehensible, doesn't it? How many times in meetings do you hear "That'll never work" or "We've tried it before, it won't work"?

Unfortunately, this phenomenon can blind us to exploring new ideas and opportunities, inhibiting creative solutions to anticipated or real problems. Too often we try to visualize the future by looking through past old paradigms. Remember these outmoded paradigms?

- The 4-minute mile will never be broken.
- We'll never put a man on the moon.
- Computerized learning will never catch on.
- The Japanese will always create inferior products.

Today, you will find that every one of these paradigms has been broken. To break them, individuals had to hold different viewpoints and place their determination and efforts behind their convictions. Here are some examples of the roles paradigms have played in organizational life over time:

- No one saw the revolutionary impact of the personal computer until Steven Jobs created Apple computers.
- American companies did not fully welcome the total quality management (TQM) movement until Japan, introduced to it by an American named Demming, demonstrated tremendous success with it. Demming's previous attempts to promote TQM principles had been futile.

In all of these examples, a new or different paradigm was introduced. Hence, a "paradigm shift" occurred. Often these new ideas were generated from outside an existing organizational structure. This occurred largely because outside individuals, or groups, were not limited by existing paradigms. When paradigms shift, everyone goes back to zero and competition is fair game. It's as if an entirely new game with new rules is created with all players being equal and required to start at the same place. The winner is usually the one who seizes the opportunity to plunge ahead. Consider this paradigm shift:

- Americans were once predominant in the camera industry. Later, the Japanese developed a higher-quality, lower-cost camera that earned them a reputation for manufacturing the best cameras in the world. In time, the Germans designed superior-quality telephoto and telescopic lenses to be used with Japanese cameras. As a result, the Germans captured a major segment of the camera industry from the Japanese.

Can you think of others?

_____

_____

_____

_____

_____

_____

_____

_____

3

■ Exercise 3.2

Explore some paradigm shifts in your own profession in the space below.

Former Paradigm	Paradigm Shift
_____	_____
_____	_____
_____	_____
_____	_____
_____	_____

Review the paradigms you listed in Exercise 3.1.

1. How many of these could possibly shift?

_____

_____

_____

_____

_____

2. What impact might such shifts have on you, your department, and your organization?

_____

_____

_____

_____

_____

OVERCOMING PARADIGM PARALYSIS

What can you do about paradigms as they relate to initiating and embracing needed changes in your organization? How can you move yourself forward when you filter ideas through rules and regulations formulated only from past experience? Here are some useful guidelines for you to consider:

- Recognize that paradigms are common.
- Realize that paradigms can be useful in helping to locate important problems and can provide you with a set of rules to begin solving them.
- Realize that paradigms can be detrimental by blocking you from new ideas or solutions, creating the disease of uncertainty, or paradigm paralysis.
- Recognize present paradigms and be willing to go beyond them.
- Value and allow for differences as well as risk taking. There may be great gain in doing so. People who create new paradigms are usually outsiders.
- If you are attempting to introduce new paradigms, be committed and courageous. Others holding old paradigms may not easily embrace your ideas or demonstrate trust.
- Realize that you can choose to change your own set of rules and regulations by altering your paradigms. Be optimistic about the future and embrace new opportunities.*

---

* For more on paradigms, see the works of Joel Barker, including "Discovering the Future: The Business of Paradigms," a film distributed by Chart House Films.

■ Exercise 3.3

1. What elements in your workplace, which may seem impossible today, could be further developed or accomplished to create new opportunities?

_____

_____

_____

_____

_____

2. What ideas do you have for making this happen? Feel free to ask others so you can avoid being frozen by your own paradigms.

_____

_____

_____

_____

_____

3

Chapter 3 Checkpoints

✓ Organizational paradigms are sets of rules and regulations that establish boundaries for making decisions.

✓ When incoming information does not fit our existing paradigms, you tend to either screen it out or change it until it does. Often this phenomenon blinds us to new opportunities for change.

✓ Paradigm shifts occur when new ideas, often initiated from the outside, begin to supersede old ideas. When these shifts occur, everyone goes back to zero, and competition is fair game.

✓ Paradigm paralysis can be overcome by being aware of existing paradigms and stretching beyond them.

4 | Exploring the Human Dynamics of Change

This chapter will help you to:

- Identify and plan for the predictable forces in change.
- Understand how the quest for equilibrium affects behavior.
- Learn what your natural abilities and limitations are for adapting to change.
- Recognize, acknowledge, and manage different preferences for change.

The Visionary Memo

It was Friday, June 15, at 4:00 PM An urgent interoffice memo from Paul Johnson, president of Vision Corporation, had just been issued to all employee mailboxes. All departments had been briefed by their respective managers to expect this memo. Employees had been given none of the particulars about it, but rumors were already flying as they anxiously awaited its arrival.

Molly Branigan, one of Vision's managers, who had no more information than anyone else in the organization, was one of the first to read the memo. It read as follows:

4

> TO: All Personnel
>
> FROM: Paul Johnson, President
>
> DATE: June 15
>
> RE: Company Status Update
>
> As you all know, Vision Corporation has been experiencing financial difficulties. In order to address these difficulties, Vision will be merging with another similar corporation, Bywright. This plan will be effective July 1 of this year. While it may call for some changes from us, I believe that this move represents a wonderful growth opportunity for the company as a whole. I look forward to your ongoing cooperation and support.

Questions to Consider

1. How do you think Molly, or other managers, might react to this memo?

_____

_____

_____

2. How do you think the general employee population will react to this memo?

_____

_____

_____

3. How would *you* react to this memo?

_____

_____

_____

4. What problems do you see in the president's approach?

_____

_____

_____

5. If you were the president of Vision Corporation, what would you have done differently?

_____

_____

_____

PLANNING FOR THE PREDICTABLE FORCES IN CHANGE

Regardless of how a particular change is viewed—positively or negatively—some predictable forces can be counted on when change is introduced. As you responded to questions 1, 2, and 3 from the chapter opening vignette, you may have already discovered some of them.

■ Exercise 4.1

Visualize yourself in an organization that is undergoing traumatic change. You have just been called to a managers' meeting for a briefing. The following announcement is made by the company's chief executive officer:

> As you know, our organization is in serious financial difficulty, and I have been working with our board of directors on recovery plans. Unfortunately, because of our immediate financial need, we will have to streamline the organization. We will be taking steps to restructure and downsize. Plans for this are currently underway and will be announced once they are complete. I appreciate your ongoing support and thank you for coming.

1. What are the first thoughts that enter your mind after hearing this announcement?

_____

_____

_____

_____

_____

2. What questions would need to be addressed before you could give the organization your support in this change effort?

_____

_____

_____

_____

_____

As you completed this exercise, questions concerning personal job security, roles and responsibilities, alteration of routines, and skills and abilities to accomplish the change may have come up. The political dynamics of change—including issues such as who's guiding the ship, jockeying for power, repositioning, assessing individual pros and cons, and sizing up supporters and nonsupporters—usually are considered next. Finally, concern for the impact on the overall organizational culture is considered. Any complex change can affect an organization's culture, which in turn will affect how people live and work within an organization.

These three concerns are illustrated in the following model of change dynamics:

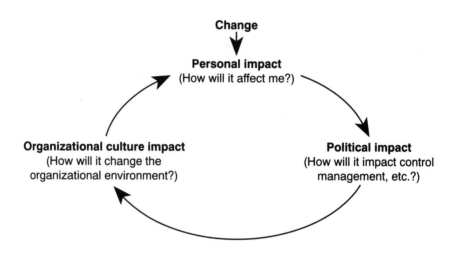

As this model illustrates, a person's first reaction to change is generally personal in nature. Individual concerns need to be heard and addressed *before* people can fully support a change, much less embrace an organizational vision. How many times have you seen the infamous "visionary" memo about a change end up in a circular file or wastepaper basket? These memos, while well-intentioned, are too general in nature and often address aspects of change that most people are unable to visualize or identify with early on. When personal needs are ignored, the greater overall organizational vision cannot be seen or understood.

Note that the model of change just illustrated depicts a *continuous cycle.* Steer well away from managing change as if it had a beginning and an end. Don't carelessly use phrases such as "Just hang in there with me; it'll be over soon." Phrases like this set up an expectation that once you get through a change, you won't be asked to change again. Instead, you should communicate that change is constant and necessary for the continued good health of the organization.

THE QUEST FOR EQUILIBRIUM

Another important human dynamic in the change process is the quest for balance or equilibrium.

■ Exercise 4.2

Stand on your toes on one foot for as long as you can. Note your reactions and behaviors at the start of, during, and after this task.

1. What did you need to change as you progressed through the exercise?

_____

_____

_____

_____

_____

2. What did you do to cope with your sense of instability?

_____

_____

_____

_____

_____

3. How does this exercise relate to change?

_____

_____

_____

_____

_____

When change is introduced, as in this exercise, stability is thrown off. Whether real or perceived, adherence to the status quo creates a sense of inner stability and balance. Only until you have practiced and become equally familiar with a new way will you begin to feel comfortable. As a manager, you need to create as much ongoing stability as possible in order for your employees to attain a sense of balance within themselves and their organizational environment. While hardly scientific, the following formula depicts this concept well:

Balance = Change + Stability/Support

When you consider what causes instability, you can work to prevent or reduce its impact by proactive support planning. Your plans might include delivering clear directions and expectations, building confidence, providing new skills training, and allowing enough time for employees to adjust to the changes. As is often said, "You can't eat an elephant in one bite."

Be sure to pay attention to when and why people overcompensate during a change process. How often have you witnessed the new learner on the computer saving multiple copies of a document on disk as well as paper? What are the unspoken needs for support that are being demonstrated by this behavior? If you observe people carefully at the early stages of a change process, you can pick up vital clues for selecting and providing appropriate support. However, always check your assumptions with the individuals affected. Your ability to provide appropriate and timely support will do much to facilitate a smooth transition.

YOUR NATURAL ABILITIES AND LIMITATIONS

Complete the following exercise before proceeding further with this discussion.

Exercise 4.3

Task A:

Write your full name in the space below.

_____

Task B:

Now, use your opposite hand to write your name.

_____

1. What were your reactions, verbal and nonverbal, as you participated in this exercise? (Compare task A with task B.)

_____
_____
_____
_____
_____

2. How did you feel about what you accomplished in task B?

_____

_____

_____

_____

_____

3. Regardless of your feelings about task B, were you able to complete it?

_____

_____

4. What might occur if you had the opportunity to practice task B many times?

_____

_____

_____

_____

_____

As you moved from task A to task B, you were presented with a change and a new challenge. As a natural response, you may have experienced a feeling that you couldn't do it. Other typical responses to this exercise range from feeling extremely humbled, embarrassed, frustrated, or defeated. Unless you are ambidextrous, you probably also felt that the quality of task B compared to task A was diminished, that it took more time, and that it was more difficult to accomplish. You may have discovered that, despite your uneasiness, you were able to complete this task. If given the opportunity to practice, you could most likely increase quality, decrease production time, and feel more comfortable.

Most people have the ability to adapt and change no matter how uncomfortable that change may seem at first. As a manager, you must give employees opportunities to stretch, develop, and grow, and as a role model, to demand the same of yourself.

MANAGING DIFFERENT PREFERENCES

In Chapter 2, you discovered your own feelings about and reactions to change. Everyone deals differently with change. All people have different qualities and skills that are reflected in their natural preferences. These preferences can range from a preference for maintenance (i.e., maintaining the status quo) to a preference for change (i.e., exploring new opportunities). Working in harmony, a sense of balance *can* be achieved.

As a leader, you need to acknowledge and appreciate these differences in yourself and in others. Accommodate individual differences pertaining to the pace of change. Rarely does anyone prefer only one or the other—maintenance or change—all of the time.

Exercise 4.4

Consider a change effort that you wish to implement. Based on your past experience with change and the exercises that you have completed thus far, summarize your thoughts regarding the anticipated human dynamics of this change.

Change Project:

Natural Forces in Change

1. *Personal Impact:*

_____

2. *Political Impact:*

_____

3. *Organizational Culture Impact:*

_____

Quest for Equilibrium

1. What might throw people off balance?

_____

_____

2. What supports can you provide to help people achieve a sense of stability?

_____

_____

Ability to Adapt and Change

1. How well do you feel people will adapt and change?

_____

_____

2. What factors could make it difficult or easy for them to change?

_____

_____

_____

Natural Preference

1. What do you believe is your own and your individual employees' natural preference: change, maintenance, or somewhere in between? (Explain why.)

_____

_____

_____

2. How can you adjust your own management or work style to accommodate natural preference differences among people with whom you work?

_____

_____

_____

Chapter 4 Checkpoints

✓ When a change is introduced, three predictable forces come into play: personal impact, political dynamics impact, and organizational culture impact.

✓ Change often creates a sense of imbalance which, whether real or perceived, must be recognized and stabilized to achieve equilibrium.

✓ Most people have the ability to adapt to change. As a manager and role model, you must stretch yourself as well as those you work with to develop and grow.

✓ Each person has a natural preference—change or maintenance. Leaders must develop and utilize both to be successful.

5 | Types of Change and Their Impact

This chapter will help you to:

- Identify the three types of change and their characteristics.
- Understand how the responses to change vary according to the type of change involved.
- Develop plans for managing each type of change.

Lifeforce Lessons

Biodynamics is an established biotech firm. Like other firms of its type, it comprises mostly research scientists. For the past 10 years it has experienced tremendous progress as new products have been researched, developed, and submitted for drug trials. Its best and most promising product, Lifeforce, is beginning to take off. At the same time, other products, still far behind, are creating tremendous strain on existing company resources. This fact, however, is not well known to others in the company.

After reviewing the annual report, the company president, Werner Freilich, realized he had to make some changes. He had hoped that the other new products would also take off and therefore delayed any research and development policy changes for a number of years. For Lifeforce's market potential to be fully realized, he now knew that he would have to stop diverting company resources.

Freilich called for a meeting with all of his managers. He announced:

"We can no longer go on existing as we have been. The company is on the brink of bankruptcy. Lifeforce is our only hope for survival, and, in order for us to realize its full potential, resources will have to be reallocated. The company, as you know it, will be gone. I have decided to place all of our resources into Lifeforce. Our vision is to shift from research to manufacturing over the next two years once Lifeforce takes off. I can't tell you when or how this will happen because much of this will depend upon future developments. I ask that you brief your staff about this situation and let them know that we will keep them apprised of any future progress. I know that I can count on your support." ∎

Questions to Consider

1. What factors may have contributed to reaching this "do or die" situation—that is, changing from research to manufacturing?

_____
_____
_____

2. If you were a manager hearing this announcement, how would you respond?

_____
_____
_____

3. What, if anything, would you do differently as the president of this company?

_____
_____
_____

THREE TYPES OF CHANGE

Why do people have varying responses to change? In some cases, they seem to go with the flow, and in other cases they are traumatized. Much of this variation in response can be directly attributed to the *type* of change.

There are three major types of change: developmental, transitional, and transformational—in order of increasing impact. The chapter opening vignette depicts a classic example of transformational change. The following table identifies and compares the definitions and characteristics of these three types of change:

TYPES OF CHANGE AND THEIR CHARACTERISTICS

	Developmental	Transitional	Transformational
Definition	Doing more or better than what currently exists.	Implementation of a new state, which requires dismantling the present ways of operating and introducing new ways.	Implementation of an evolutionary new state, which requires major and often ongoing shifts in organizational strategy and vision.
Examples	■ Team building. ■ Expanding market. ■ Enhancing communication. ■ Technical expertise.	■ Reorganization. ■ New techniques. ■ New products and services. ■ New methods and procedures.	■ Mergers and acquisitions. ■ Insolvencies. ■ Major shifts in product line(s). ■ Major restructuring efforts. ■ Consolidations. ■ Total quality strategies (in some cases).
Characteristics	■ Least threatening. ■ Easiest to manage.	■ Somewhat threatening. ■ Occurs over a set period of time. ■ Usually referred to as the transition stage. ■ Future state is consciously chosen (e.g., a specific goal or end point has been established; however, you may not know how to get there).	■ Most threatening. ■ Profound and traumatic. ■ Difficult to control. ■ Future state is largely unknown until it evolves.

▪ Exercise 5.1

Think back on your own experiences. Identify some of the changes you have experienced and list them in the appropriate categories.

1. *Developmental:*

_____

_____

_____

2. *Transitional:*

_____

_____

_____

_____

_____

3. *Transformational:*

_____

_____

_____

_____

_____

CHANGE RESPONSES ACCORDING TO TYPE

To see differences among the three types of change and their impacts, complete the following exercise (and don't forget to exercise your imagination).

■ **E x e r c i s e 5 . 2**

Read the vacation scenarios below and respond to the questions that follow each one.

Scenario 1.   It is time to make your annual reservation at your vacation cottage. You have returned to this particular cottage year after year because of its location near the water. This year you have an opportunity to rent a nicer cottage, much closer to the water.

    1. Would you rent the new cottage? (Circle one.)   Yes   Maybe   No

    2. What factors influenced your decision?

_____

_____

_____

_____

_____

3. How difficult was this change request for you? (Explain your response.)

_____

_____

_____

_____

_____

Scenario 2.   This year another vacation is being planned. You have the time and resources to take it. The destination is Aruba. However, some of the details still have to be worked out. You don't know at this point how you're going to get there (e.g., boat, plane, etc.) or how long you may stay at various places on the island.

1. Would you go on this vacation? (Circle one.)   Yes   Maybe   No

2. What factors influenced your decision?

_____

_____

_____

_____

_____

3. How difficult was this change request for you? (Explain your response.)

_____

_____

_____

_____

_____

Scenario 3:   It's time for vacation number three. This year's vacation is the mystery tour. You don't know where you're going, how you're going to get there, or what you'll be doing ahead of time. You could be panning for gold, digging ditches, or whatever. You won't find out until you get there.

1. Would you go on this vacation? (Circle one.)   Yes   Maybe   No

2. What factors influenced your decision?

_____

_____

_____

_____

_____

3. How difficult was this change request for you? (Explain your response.)

_____

_____

_____

_____

_____

Summary Question

What do these scenarios and your responses to them tell you about change?

_____

_____

_____

_____

_____

You have just experienced three different types of changes. Scenario 1 was an example of developmental change. For most, the new cottage represents a developmental change or an improvement over what currently exists. Scenario 2 was an example of transitional change. Key to this situation is that you have a destination or endpoint, although you may not know how you are going to get there. Scenario 3, an example of transformational change, is an evolving change. Not only do you not know how you are going, but you do not even know where you are going until you arrive.

Compare your responses to the scenarios. You may find that your interest in going on vacation decreased as you moved through the scenarios. In some cases, you may have found that you were on the fence and that more information about particular accommodations might have made the situation more palatable. If you have a natural love for adventure and generally enjoy the challenge of change, you probably discovered that your interest in the vacations increased as you moved from scenario 1 to scenario 3.

Among others who have participated in this exercise, the percentage of willing vacationers drops off markedly as you move from developmental change to transformational change. For example, among a group of 20 people, you will usually find only 1 or 2 who want to sign up for vacation three. Generally, these are people who gravitate to change, finding it both exciting and rewarding.

This phenomenon occurs as a natural response to change. Regardless of the situation, most people like to feel some sense of control or stability—for example, where they are going and even how they are going to get there. If their natural preference is maintenance, these factors become increasingly important. In transformational change, many of these questions cannot be answered at the start, because the change itself evolves as time goes on.

Organizations that have lived too long in the mode of "If it's not broken, why fix it" often find themselves thrown into transformational change as a survival tactic. Far too often, this change is too much too late for an organization to accomplish without significant and possible irreparable damage. Other organizations undergo transformational changes as a result of external forces. Some of these may have been predictable, planned for, and worked on as developmental or transitional changes, thus preventing the need for transformational change. Others may not have. Examples of external forces include drastic economic shifts that affect business decisions, new regulatory policies or procedures, paradigm shifts, and so on.

PLANNING IMPLICATIONS

Developmental Change

Developmental change requires systems-level support to survive. Generally, people respond to developmental change favorably, because it is viewed as an improvement to an existing state. If, however, people do not respond favorably, and you believe that the change is still important, you will have to work with those affected until they are equally convinced or at least willing to try it. One of the best ways to gain acceptance to any change, of course, is to enable ideas for change to originate and develop from the individuals affected. If this is not possible because a change decision has already been made, at the very least, involve people in implementation planning.

Transitional Change

The key to managing transitional change lies in its name, "transition." How effectively you manage the transitional process will affect not only receptivity, but understanding, acceptance, and final adoption. What creates uncertainty is the process of moving from a known way of doing things to a new, often unfamiliar way. Although you may have a specific goal in mind, you may not know exactly how to get there. Generally, this type of change requires patience, time, and effort to be fully realized.

Effective two-way communication is vital to assisting people in the transition process. Be clear about the change, identify similarities (if they exist) and/or differences between current and new ways, report regularly on the status of the change or progress made (even when there may be no new news), and acknowledge effort and success. If milestones to measure success are set, be sure everyone knows what they are and whether they have been met. If milestones *won't* be met, communicate the reasons and revise plans accordingly, because people will be motivated by reaching the milestones. Thus, setting milestones affects momentum and affects end results.

Transformational Change

Transformational change is the most difficult to manage. It requires great skill and should by no means be undertaken by a beginner. Many of your most vivid and negative memories of change no doubt come from transformational changes that have been mismanaged. These memories are incorporated into your frame of reference, greatly influencing how you perceive and cope with future change.

As a manager you must clearly communicate change in organizational strategy and vision. Consider the caterpillar turning into a butterfly. Who would have thought, without knowing ahead of time, that this could happen? In organizational life, this metamorphic phenomenon requires visualizing your organization as something totally different from what you have known or recognized it to be.

With transformational change, it is not possible or desirable to provide people with an end goal (as you should in transitional change). The transformational change itself is evolutionary, often dramatically affected by various steps along the way. Unrealized promises merely build disappointment, distrust, and increased resistance. Your challenge is to manage the ambiguity and lead your organization toward a moving target. Remember the mystery vacation in Exercise 5.2? Most people don't want to sign up for it when given the choice, and so it is with transformational change.

One of the best ways to manage transformational change is to educate people about what it is, why they feel the way they do, and why you may not be able to answer all the questions they may have. Communicating like this builds a foundation of understanding and trust from which to move forward.

General Planning Considerations

5

As you plan for change, anticipate and address the following issues:

- How to educate people about change.
- How to create effective two-way communication.
- How to purposefully select a desired future state (when and if this is possible).
- How to provide for continuous quality and service while changes are in progress.
- How to build momentum and commitment necessary to set changes in motion.
- How to orchestrate changes within specific time frames.
- How to deal with human responses to change—anxiety, resistance, excitement, and so on.

Exercise 5.3

Visualize a change that you would like to make in your organization.

1. Describe the change.

_____

_____

_____

_____

_____

2. Is it developmental, transitional, or transformational? (Explain.)

_____

_____

_____

_____

_____

3. How do you think people will feel about and react to this change?

_____

_____

_____

_____

_____

4. Based upon what you know about this type of change and change planning in general, develop some preliminary ideas for its implementation.

_____

_____

_____

_____

_____

Chapter 5 Checkpoints

✓ There are three types of change: developmental, transitional, and transformational.

✓ Developmental change is the easiest change to manage and generally entails improving an existing state or way of doing things.

✓ Transitional change is somewhat threatening as it requires moving through a process of dismantling current procedures and replacing them with new and more desirable ones.

✓ Because of its evolutionary nature, transformational change requires managing ambiguity and leading an organization toward a moving target.

6 | Managing Change as a Process

This chapter will help you to:

- Understand change as a process.
- Identify key areas of concern for managing transition.
- Develop strategies and tactics for managing the change process.

You Can Bank on Change

With the economy greatly depressed, the banking industry was becoming extremely competitive. Lucille Perez, People's International Bank president, watched despairingly as more and more banks developed incentive programs to attract and increase their customer base. Free checking accounts, low-interest home equity and first-time home buyer loans, waivers of closing costs and annual credit card fees, financial planning services, automated teller machines, and extended banking hours reflected only some of the many up-and-coming innovations.

Suddenly, Lucille came up with a brilliant idea for how People's International could stay competitive. It was an idea that truly would respond to increasing customer demand for higher quality and faster service. She was so fired up about the idea that she called her division heads together that afternoon for an emergency meeting to share her plan.

Called to attention, the division heads gathered in the boardroom to listen to the new plan. Lucille presented her plan as follows:

"As you all know, other banks are taking People's International by storm. Customers right and left are being attracted away from us with new incentive programs. For us to compete, we need to really stand out above the crowd. We must offer an incentive to customers that no one else has offered before. Therefore, I am proposing that we offer a one-stop banking service to all of our customers. Rather than continuing to departmentalize our services and forcing customers to chase all around the bank, we need to start providing all services through a single contact person assigned to each customer. I believe that this will put us on the cutting edge of banking, and for this reason we'll be implementing this plan starting next week." ■

Questions to Consider

1. How do you think the division heads will respond to this change, and what concerns might they have?

_____

_____

_____

2. How would *you* respond, and what concerns would you have?

_____

_____

_____

3. How might customer service be affected when this plan *first* goes into effect?

_____

_____

_____

4. What suggestions do you have for managing this situation differently?

_____

_____

_____

CHANGE AS A PROCESS

You probably have heard of the straight-line approach to organizational change. This approach, as seen in the chapter opening vignette, suggests that you can go directly from one way of doing things to another way, as the following diagram illustrates:

$$A \longrightarrow B$$
Old way   New way

In reality, how successful might you be if you managed change in this way?

▋ E x e r c i s e   6 . 1

Think back to the last time you moved. Try to recall how you felt during those first few days in your new place. List any thoughts and feelings (positive or negative) that come into your mind.

Positive	Negative
_____	_____
_____	_____
_____	_____
_____	_____
_____	_____
_____	_____
_____	_____
_____	_____

Generally, a variety of memories crops up. Some typical examples might include:

Positive	Negative
■ I like the feeling of this new place.	■ I feel disoriented.
■ I can meet new people.	■ I miss my old friends.
■ It's more spacious.	■ I don't know where anything is.
■ I like the neighborhood better.	■ My support systems are gone.
■ Finally, I'll have more room.	■ The curtains don't look right.

This list highlights the fact that there are almost always negative elements to *any* change—not just moving. People naturally tend to cling to the familiar or established routine, making it difficult to let go of the past immediately. It's almost as if there is a gravitational pull back to what's known. Consider what might motivate you to do the following:

6

- Attend high school or college reunions.
- Sit in the same seat every week during a course, even though the seats are unassigned.
- Drive the same way to work every day, even when there are alternative routes that are just as good.

This dynamic is essential to understanding and managing human behavior in change. It is easy to develop wonderful ideas for doing things in new or different ways, but it is not possible to implement those ideas without successfully managing the people who are responsible for carrying them out. The art of managing change lies not just in how well you plan for change but in how you manage transitions and the people they impact.

KEY CONCERNS FOR MANAGING TRANSITIONS

The key concerns for managing transitions are depicted in the diagram below and consist of the following:

- How to effectively assist people in letting go of the present ways of doing things.
- How to effectively direct and manage people in their movement through the transition period.
- How to provide the necessary support for people to accept, adopt, and execute new ways of doing tasks.

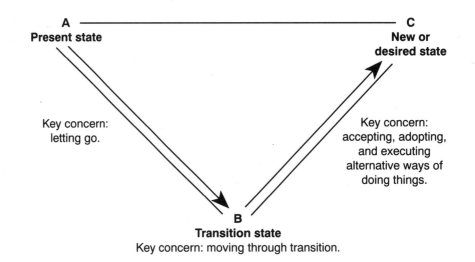

A ———————————————————————————— C
Present state   **New or desired state**

Key concern: letting go.

Key concern: accepting, adopting, and executing alternative ways of doing things.

B
Transition state
Key concern: moving through transition.

 **Exercise 6.2**

Consider the last transition you experienced and answer the following questions.

1. What was the change?

_____
_____
_____
_____
_____

2. What was the present state prior to the change?

_____
_____
_____
_____
_____

3. What was the new or desired state?

_____
_____
_____
_____
_____

4. What helped or hindered letting go of the present state?

Helping Behaviors	Hindering Behaviors
_____	_____
_____	_____
_____	_____
_____	_____
_____	_____

5. What helped or hindered smooth movement through the transition state?

Helping Behaviors	Hindering Behaviors

6. What helped or hindered accepting, adopting, and executing the new state?

Helping Behaviors	Hindering Behaviors

STRATEGIES AND TACTICS

The chart on page 57 outlines characteristics and key concerns related to each phase of change along with recommended strategies and tactics for coping with them. While this will provide you with some general guidelines, keep in mind that specific and varying individual needs as well as abilities will need to be considered and addressed.

Listed below and on page 58 are some additional ideas for managing the change process.

Present State

Goal: To move people away from the present state.

Ideas:

- Acknowledge what's unfinished.

CHARACTERISTICS, STRATEGIES, AND TACTICS FOR MANAGING THE CHANGE PROCESS*

	Change Stages		
	Present State (Frozen) ⟶	**Transition State (Unfreezing)** ⟶	**New State (Refreezing)**
Key Concern	**Letting Go**	**Confusion to Understanding**	**Understanding to Actualizing**
Characteristic Behaviors	Clinging to the status quo; gravitational pull to the past.	Guilt, self-absorption, rumors, conflict sabotage, stress, blame, increased perceived value of status quo.	Tentative risk-taking, need for continued support and practice.
Strategy	Disconfirm and promote movement away from present state.	Encourage movement through communication, guidance, structure, confidence, and trust.	Reconfirm benefits of change; promote acceptance and adoption of new state.
Tactics for Change	1. Identify organizational problems and opportunities that cause the status quo to no longer be viable, now or in the future. 2. Highlight personal and organizational costs of not changing. Focus gains on individual or initial personal impacts. 3. Verbalize and demonstrate strong commitment to the change. 4. Reduce defensiveness about the past through open communication. 5. Detail expected changes and plans for implementation if known.	1. Reinforce need for change and focus on the future. 2. Encourage self-confidence by emphasizing capabilities for achieving change and benefits of new state. 3. Reinforce change by acknowledging and highlighting progress. 4. Provide accurate and timely information. 5. Allow those affected to be involved in planning the change and its implementation. 6. Provide necessary resources and support to succeed, including change awareness; skills training; and financial, political, and logistical support. 7. Identify supporters who can provide constancy and stability.	1. Continue to demonstrate strong support of the change. 2. Acknowledge accomplishments in moving through transition state and highlight benefits of emerging new state. 3. Provide appropriate rewards. 4. Exercise appropriate consequence management for those who are unwilling to change, including coaching, transfer, or discharge.
Tips	Allow people to express their feelings and concerns openly and be empathetic. Realize that change for some is very difficult.	Listen for concerns and feelings. Build trust through two-way communication and support.	Allow for practice and mistakes. Create ladders of support for people; follow up.
What to Avoid	Whitewashing—e.g., "It's easy. You'll get over it. You shouldn't feel this way."	Focusing on organizational needs and not individual needs—e.g., issuing vague visionary memos that speak only to organizational concerns or gains.	Asking everyone to carry the flag right away. For some it takes time. Changing too much, too fast.

6

* *Source:* Adapted from *Managing Organizational Change: Implementation Planning Procedure*, p. 16, Copyright 1990, with permission of Daryl R. Conner, ODR, Inc., 2900 Chamblee–Tucker Rd., Atlanta, GA 30341.

- Celebrate endings (e.g., ceremonies, company newsletter, obituary columns, etc.).
- Allow people some distance.
- Allow people to vent.
- Listen and watch for support-request clues.
- Spend time with those affected.

Transition State

Goal: To facilitate smooth movement through the transition state.

Ideas:

- Create transition teams (e.g., transition-monitoring teams made up of one sector of your organization).
- Seek information about how people are reacting to the change.
- Observe—look for overcompensating behaviors and provide support.
- Provide transitional seminars; acknowledge how people are feeling and engage them in problem-solving as necessary.

New State

Goal: To accept, adopt, and execute the new state.

Ideas:

- Involve people in achieving the new goals of the company.
- Demonstrate success (e.g., rewards, celebration, newsletters, etc.).
- Create a "futures" task force.
- Reward accomplishment (e.g., self-funded profit sharing, increased involvement in which the receivers would be interested (ask them), merit raises, educational perks, employee suggestion programs).

Exercise 6.3

Consider a change that you would like to make in your organization. Develop some preliminary plans for managing the change process during each of the three phases.

1. Identify the change goal.

_____

_____

_____

_____

2. Describe present state.

_____

_____

_____

_____

3. Describe new or desired state.

_____

_____

_____

_____

4. List your implementation plans.
Phase I (Present State):

_____

_____

_____

_____

_____

Phase II (Transition State):

_____

_____

_____

_____

_____

Phase III (New or Desired State):

_____

_____

_____

_____

_____

Be sure to check your ideas against some of the suggestions made throughout this chapter. Obtain feedback from your employees, peers, and managers to fine tune your ideas.

Chapter 6 Checkpoints

✓ Change is a process of moving from a present state through a transitional state to a new state.

✓ Key areas of concern in managing transitions are as follows:
- How to effectively assist people in letting go of the present state.
- How to effectively direct and manage movement through the transition state.
- How to provide the necessary support for acceptance, adoption, and execution of the new or desired state.

✓ There are many strategies and tactics for managing transitions, but they all require that you listen, hear, respond, and lead.

7

Critical Roles in the Change Process

This chapter will help you to:

- Identify critical roles and relationships in the change process.
- Learn how synergy can influence change and its implementation.
- Develop guidelines for how critical roles can support the change process.

The Black Hole Syndrome

It was Friday morning, 10:00 AM. Ten division heads of Families First Health Care, Inc., a health maintenance organization, gathered around the boardroom table for their bi-weekly meeting with the president. An agenda, which said at the top "Planning for Our Future," was distributed to all participants. Diana Packowski, president of Families First Health Care, kicked off the meeting.

"As we all know, the demand for providing high-quality, low-cost health care services is skyrocketing. Not only are our customers asking for this, but new government regulations and reimbursement structures are requiring it. After reviewing our last quarterly report, it has become apparent that we can no longer continue operating as we have in the past. For this reason, I have decided that we will be launching a total quality management [TQM] effort. Each of you will be held accountable for this effort within your respective divisions. It will be your responsibility to assess what's needed and to see that TQM is fully implemented in six months."

True to form, the meeting carried on and concluded with a one-way dialogue from the president. Division heads left the meeting shaking their heads and mumbling, "Here we go again . . . I can't believe it . . . Another 'hurry up and wait.' "

For the next few months, division heads dutifully struggled with this new charge. They informed their department heads and expected them to carry the ball. Most were as unfamiliar with TQM as they themselves were and had no idea where to begin. Requests for training were denied due to "budget constraints." Follow-up discussions with the president regarding this task were nonexistent, and future division meetings were dedicated to new and "equally important" organizational priorities.

Six months passed. Division heads were once again assembled for their biweekly meeting. An agenda that read "Status Reports on TQM Implementation" was circulated. Division heads were aghast, thinking the matter had long been forgotten. As the president called for reports, there was little or nothing for them to say. It became painfully apparent that the TQM effort had gone down the proverbial black hole. ■

■ Questions to Consider

1. What factors contributed to the change failure (i.e., the nonimplementation of the TQM effort)?

_____

_____

_____

2. How could each of the individuals or groups have worked more effectively to achieve the change?

_____

_____

_____

3. What steps would you take to prevent this situation from occurring again and to resolve the current situation?

_____

_____

_____

WHAT ARE THE CRITICAL ROLES IN THE CHANGE PROCESS?

Critical to the successful implementation of any change effort are the roles people play and how well they are carried out. There are five major roles in the change process:

1. Initiating sponsors.
2. Sustaining sponsors.
3. Agents.
4. Targets.
5. Advocates.

Initiating and Sustaining Sponsors

Change sponsors are individuals or groups of people who legitimize a change. Traditionally, sponsorship came from a company president or top-level manager. Initiating sponsors usually start the change effort, but sustaining sponsors are the ones who often have more direct involvement in overseeing the change process. In today's empowered workplace, sponsorship can come from other levels of a company. Critical to sponsors' success is their recognition as credible sources of sponsorship.

In the chapter opening vignette, the president acted as the initiating sponsor, charging the division heads with the role of sustaining sponsors. As demonstrated in this scenario, ineffective sponsorship can be caused by failure to establish and demonstrate commitment to organizational priorities, to provide necessary information and resources, and to select and prepare sustaining sponsors adequately. Omissions such as these can result in no change, superficial change, short-term change, or distorted change. In short, changes can drop into a "black hole," wasting valuable time and resources. Results of ineffective sponsorship are illustrated below.

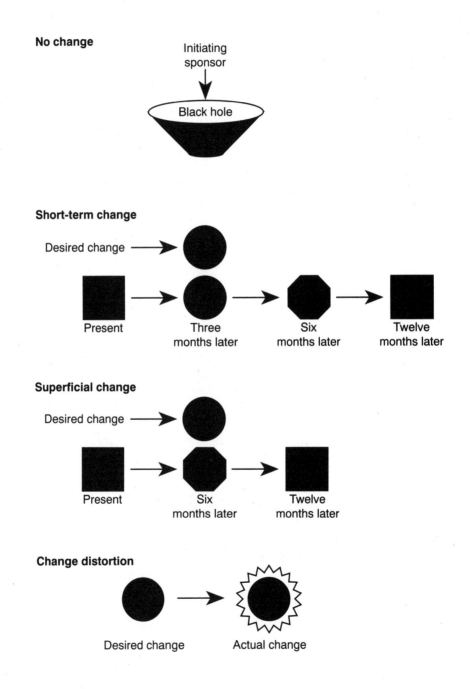

No change

Initiating sponsor

Black hole

Short-term change

Desired change

Present

Three months later

Six months later

Twelve months later

Superficial change

Desired change

Present

Six months later

Twelve months later

Change distortion

Desired change

Actual change

Conversely, building a solid foundation of support for a change through sustaining sponsors has a much greater likelihood of success. Providing this type of support at each level of the change effort has a positive and cascading effect on the change process, as shown in the following illustration.

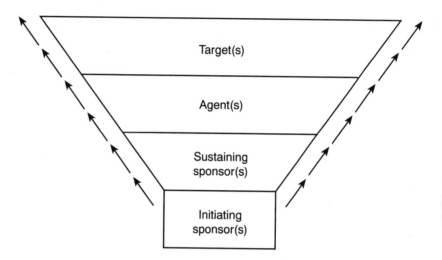

Agents

Change agents are individuals or groups of people who are responsible for implementing a change. The agent may be a manager leading her direct reports in a change or a nonmanager who has the authority and responsibility to carry out a change through the work of others.

In the chapter opening vignette, department heads were charged with this role. Like sponsors, agents must have a clear understanding of how to plan for and manage change effectively. With regard to any specific change project, they must also have as much information as possible about a change (e.g., what, where, when, why, and how), its organizational priority, their roles in the process, ongoing support, and resources for planning and implementation.

Targets

Change targets are individuals or groups of people who must realize or actually do the changing. They include any and all groups or individuals who are directly affected by the change and who must change in some way.

In the chapter opening vignette, the TQM effort went into the black hole before it ever reached the level of the departmental employee. If the effort had not failed, the role of change target would have been assigned to the departmental employee. It is critical for targets to know what is expected of them, how they can be involved in the planning and implementation phases, and what support and resources will be made available to them.

Advocates

Change advocates are individuals or groups of people who want to achieve a change but who do not possess the legitimate power to make it happen. For example, they could include a design engineer who must implement a product change through a managing supervisor, or a manager who would like to implement a change in a department outside of her usual authority, which could reap benefits for her own department.

In the chapter opening vignette, a division head recommending organizationwide implementation of TQM would represent such a role. Again, clarification of the change itself (i.e., what, why, how, etc.); establishment of roles and responsibilities in the change process; and identification of existing and needed knowledge, resources, and support are all critical factors for effectively managing and implementing change.

CRITICAL ROLE RELATIONSHIPS

There are many different structures for how the critical roles associated with change interrelate, forming several different relationships. The most common are the following:

1. Direct reporting relationships.
2. Facilitating relationships.
3. Advocating relationships.

These role relationships are depicted in the following illustrations:

Direct reporting relationships (linear approach)

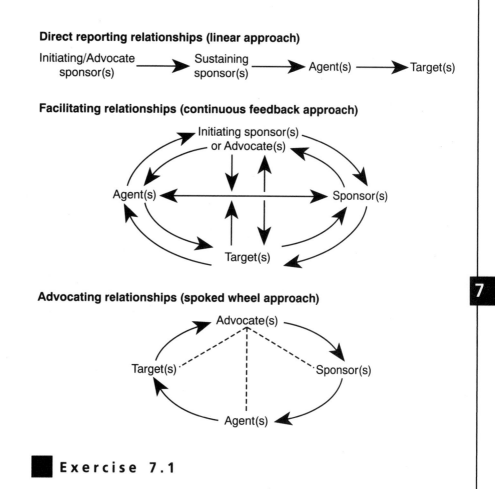

Facilitating relationships (continuous feedback approach)

Advocating relationships (spoked wheel approach)

7

■ Exercise 7.1

Consider a specific change project that you would like to see implemented in your workplace. This may be a project that you identified in previous chapters, or it may be an entirely different one.

1. Identify the change project.

_____

_____

_____

2. Identify the critical change roles.

Sponsor(s) (initiating):

_____

_____

_____

Sponsor(s) (sustaining):

_____

_____

_____

Agent(s):

_____

_____

_____

Targets(s):

_____

_____

_____

Advocate(s):

_____

_____

_____

3. What is *your* role in the change process?

_____

_____

_____

_____

_____

4. How will these roles interrelate with one another in the change process (i.e., direct reporting, facilitating, or advocating)?

_____

_____

_____

_____

_____

SYNERGY AND CHANGE

One of the most effective ways to implement and manage organizational change is for sponsors, agents, targets, and advocates to work together in a synergistic process. Synergy is the process of individuals or groups of people working together in such a way that (1) the total is greater than the sum of its individual parts and (2) the organizational benefits derived are greater than the amount of resources consumed. This requires people to work together interdependently to establish and reach a common goal. Critical to this approach is that the overall goal or task is more important than the individuals and their respective personal agendas.

To achieve synergy, key individuals in a change effort must be willing and able to effectively do the following:

- **Interact** with one another toward the accomplishment of a common goal.
- **Listen, hear, understand,** and **appreciate differences** in one another (i.e., value diversity).
- **Integrate** or merge diverse ideas.
- **Implement** these ideas by initiating and completing action plans.

The synergistic approach will significantly improve the quality of change ideas and implementation plans, significantly increase acceptance and commitment to a change effort, and, as a result, significantly decrease resistance.

Exercise 7.2

Refer back to your change project in Exercise 7.1 and answer the following questions.

1. What level of synergy exists between these individuals or groups now?

_____

_____

_____

_____

2. What can be done to increase and sustain the level of synergy before, during, and after your change effort?

_____

_____

_____

_____

SUPPORTING THE CHANGE PROCESS

As you have learned, various change roles and their interrelationships have a dramatic effect on the outcome of a change effort. Here are some useful guidelines for how each of these roles can effectively support a change process.*

Initiating Sponsor Role

1. Carefully assess, weigh, and prioritize the potential positive and negative impacts on the organization as well as required resources before initiating a change.
2. Establish a management structure for all key sustaining sponsors, agents, and targets that carefully considers both positive and negative consequences of the change.
3. Establish commitment and educate a cascading network of sustaining sponsors between you and the target population to ensure continued support of the change.
4. Clarify your role and the roles of others in the change process.
5. Communicate change priorities to the organization fully.
6. Evaluate and develop your own skills and abilities as a sponsor, as well as those of the sustaining sponsor(s) below you. (See also sustaining sponsor roles 4, 5, 6, and 7.)

Sustaining Sponsor Role

1. Communicate change priorities and resource allocations.
2. Clarify roles in the change process.
3. Establish commitment and educate change agents.

---

* Material on pages 70–71 adapted from *Optimum Performance for the Key Roles*, pp. 1–6, Copyright 1993, with permission of Daryl R. Conner, ODR, Inc., 2900 Chamblee–Tucker Rd., Atlanta, GA 30341.

4. Ensure the use of synergistic approaches in order to support and implement change effectively.

5. Provide the appropriate resources—logistical, financial, and political—necessary to carry out a change project as a demonstration of your commitment and support.

6. Assess and plan for the level of resistance and support expected from those affected by the change.

7. Use and reinforce effective change management skills throughout the change process.

Agent Role

1. Clarify and develop role responsibilities with key players.

2. Assess your own skills and abilities as a change agent on an ongoing basis. Use this information to talk with sponsor(s) about your role and to further develop your skills.

3. Assess the change project and, later, prepare an implementation plan. Be sure that you have communicated this plan to your sponsor(s) and that it has been agreed upon ahead of time.

4. Implement and follow through on your plan. Educate and gain commitment from targets.

5. Facilitate ongoing feedback from targets and sponsors regarding progress and potential or real problems related to the change effort.

6. Provide all necessary resources and support.

7. Identify and manage resistance.

Target Role

1. Determine reasons for change.

2. Discuss your questions or concerns about the change with appropiate advocate(s), agent(s), and sponsor(s).

3. Gain clarity about what is expected of you, how the change may affect your role(s), and any consequent management structure that may affect you.

4. How will dynamics be affected by the change? Will you be able to influence change? How can you contribute to a synergistic process?

Advocate Role

1. Define what you want to change and create criteria to measure success.

2. Identify key targets who must accommodate the change.

3. Clarify your role and the desired roles of others. Identify and educate others who must support the change and gain their commitment.

4. Evaluate the necessary and current skill level for managing change among each of the key players or groups. Provide appropriate resources and support.

5. Utilize synergy and effective change management skills.

■ Exercise 7.3

Refer to the change project that you identified in Exercise 7.1. Develop some initial ideas for how the various roles can work together to plan for and implement this change successfully. (Please consider the role guidelines just discussed.)

_____

_____

_____

_____

_____

Chapter 7 Checkpoints

✓ There are five key roles in the change process: initiating sponsors, sustaining sponsors, agents, targets, and advocates.

✓ The use of synergy in a change process will greatly improve the quality of change ideas and implementation strategies, increase acceptance and commitment to change, and, therefore, decrease resistance.

✓ Each of the five change roles, whether represented by individuals or groups, has distinct responsibilities that contribute to and are critical to the overall success of a change effort.

8 | Strategic Planning Considerations

This chapter will help you to:

- Identify the costs of failing to manage change.
- Establish criteria for evaluating and measuring change success.
- Understand how patterns in the change process apply to planning.
- Identify change implementation barriers and bridges.

Hard Times

Hartley Hospital was a 50-year-old unionized community hospital, serving primarily inner-city, low-income patients. Recently it had fallen on hard times due to drastic changes in reimbursement policies and a declining number of patients. Weston Hospital, a neighboring 60-year-old nonunionized hospital, serving primarily middle- to upper-income patients, was struggling with much the same issues. The cultures of these two organizations were quite different, and the struggle for survival prompted much competition between them.

After many independent efforts, the presidents of the two hospitals determined that their only means of survival was to work together. A new umbrella organization, Hartley-Weston, was formed to facilitate joint efforts. At the same time a new chairperson of the board was elected. Unfortunately, he had extremely limited experience in hospital management.

Six months passed. Both hospitals were in dire financial straits, forcing them to officially merge. The newly elected chairperson of the board emerged as the new president over both hospitals. To ease tensions, he promised, "There will be no lay-offs as a result of the merger." Both presidents were left in place; however, their titles were changed to chief executive officers, and they were disempowered.

After two months it became clear that downsizing was necessary, but employees would have ample advance notice of layoffs. Finally, the restructuring announcement came, and instead of ample notice, senior managers, who were laid off, were directed to clear out in three hours. Panic, anger, and fear permeated the organization.

Financial conditions grew increasingly worse and it became painfully apparent that more downsizing was needed. Department managers were pitted against one another as they were plucked from their positions one by one with little or no notice. Critical planning priorities were pushed aside. Morale was at an all-time low, newspapers were having a field day, the community lost all confidence in Hartley-Weston's effort, and employees were leaving faster than they could be replaced. Finances continued to plummet, leaving Hartley-Weston gasping for survival as it faced ever-increasing debt. ∎

Questions to Consider

1. What went wrong?

_____

_____

_____

2. What were some of the costs resulting from this mismanaged change?

_____

_____

_____

3. If you had managed this situation, what might you have done differently?

_____

_____

_____

4. Given the current situation, what would you do now?

_____

_____

_____

THE COSTS OF FAILURE

Managers rarely take time to consider the costs of mismanaged change before starting to implement strategic plans. Costs include the following:

- An existing problem is not solved or an opportunity is not realized.
- Time, money, and human and material resources are wasted.
- Morale declines.
- Job security is threatened.
- Future strategic directives are ignored.
- Leadership credibility declines.
- Organizational survival may be threatened.

As you can see, the cost of failure is extremely high. Leaders must think through change projects carefully before they attempt a change. The following questions are all important to consider:

- Is the timing of this change right for my organization?
- To what extent will it be supported or resisted?
- Are there other more viable alternatives?
- Will this change fit with the existing organizational culture?
- What are our current skills for managing change?
- Will the change fit organizational priorities and be supported by top management?

As these questions are addressed, it becomes apparent whether your change will be readily accepted and implemented. When major organizational resistance is determined, you can take one of three approaches: don't change, change the change, or change the organizational culture. The approach you choose should be carefully thought out and based upon the needs of the organization.

Don't Change

Timing can make or break a change situation. If there are too many organizational priorities, energy and resources to accomplish a change may be diverted, therefore limiting your chances of success. Selecting the right time for the organization can create a win-win situation, enabling other organizational priorities to be carried out successfully.

At other times it may become apparent that a change will not provide the solution you had hoped for. At this point, it is important not to move forward with your current change plans. By stopping to reconsider your plans, the costs of failure can be prevented.

Change the Change

Sometimes changes are met with major resistance because they do not appear to represent viable solutions to those affected. They must be altered in some way for greater receptivity. Involving more people (employees and managers alike) in generating change ideas and implementation strategies often can lead to a more acceptable change and increased commitment.

Change the Organization

On occasion, organizations will face major resistance to a change because of their cultures. If a change is outside of existing company paradigms (e.g., decision-making processes, past practices, written and unwritten rules, etc.), employees may be reluctant to embrace it. When such a change is truly necessary for organizational survival, realigning cultures to accept a change can be a viable solution. This can be accomplished by bringing in a transitional president, turn-around expert, or new management team. Another approach, although time-consuming, is to change organizational culture through employee training and involvement. Changing organizational culture is extremely difficult and should only be considered after careful planning.

 **Exercise 8.1**

Consider a specific change that you wish to implement.

1. Define the change.

_____

_____

_____

_____

2. Identify the specific costs of failing to manage this change well.

_____

_____

_____

_____

3. What questions might you ask and want answered to determine how receptive your organization is to this change?

_____

_____

_____

_____

4. Do your responses to these questions lead you to not change, change the change, change the organizational culture, or move ahead with your current change plans? (Explain your response.)

_____

_____

_____

_____

SUCCESS CRITERIA

What criteria can you use to determine whether or not you have been successful? While every change has its unique goals, general hallmarks of success are as follows:

- The stated goals and objectives of both the human and technical aspects of the change were achieved.
- The change project was carried out on time.

- Implementation of the change project stayed within budget.
- The change made a positive contribution or added value to the organization.

■ Exercise 8.2

Consider the change that you identified in Exercise 8.1 and develop evaluation criteria for measuring its success.

1. State the human and technical goals and objectives for measuring the success of the change.

_____

_____

_____

_____

_____

2. What is the time frame for carrying out this project? Be sure to identify milestones along the way.

_____

_____

_____

_____

_____

3. What is the budget for this project? You may want to consider indirect costs (e.g., employee time, effects of learning curve, etc.) as well as direct costs (e.g., new equipment, training, etc.).

_____

_____

_____

_____

_____

4. What organizational benefits or added value do you expect from this change?

_____

_____

_____

_____

_____

CHANGE PATTERNS

Now that you have considered the costs of failure and how you might measure success, it is useful to examine general patterns in the change process. These patterns, as depicted in the chart on page 82, provide you with useful information regarding the sequence of change events and can be applied to any change. Becoming familiar with these patterns will help you recognize, plan for, and manage critical points in your own change process. Planning for these anticipated events will substantially reduce and sometimes eliminate change implementation problems.

As depicted in the chart, each phase, while interconnected to the next, has unique planning considerations. One of the most critical steps of all is phase III, crisis or opportunity. It is here that change problems can fester and grow out of proportion. If left unresolved, change efforts can result in self-destruction (e.g., the black hole syndrome), spiraling morale problems, increased resistance, and loss of future receptivity to change. Conversely, as problems are openly surfaced, discussed, and resolved, change efforts are propelled forward.

One very useful approach for dealing with the crisis or opportunity phase is to involve those affected by a change in prevention planning. At the very start of the change process, have them work with you to identify potential problems that may arise and develop contingency plans for dealing with them. When and if these problems arise, they no longer are held up as examples of failed change but as little bumps along the way that were both expected and planned for. Strangely enough, a positive effect can result as people discover that they had enough foresight not only to anticipate particular problems ahead of time but to prepare solutions as well.

8

MOVING THROUGH THE CHANGE PROCESS

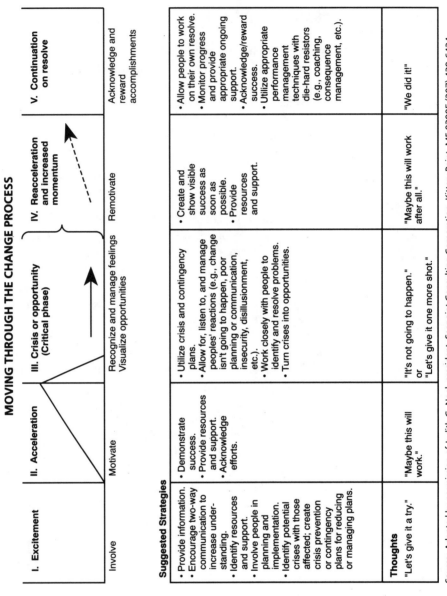

I. Excitement	II. Acceleration	III. Crisis or opportunity (Critical phase)	IV. Reacceleration and increased momentum	V. Continuation on resolve
Involve	Motivate	Recognize and manage feelings Visualize opportunities	Remotivate	Acknowledge and reward accomplishments

Suggested Strategies

I. Excitement	II. Acceleration	III. Crisis or opportunity	IV. Reacceleration	V. Continuation on resolve
• Provide information. • Encourage two-way communication to increase understanding. • Identify resources and support. • Involve people in planning and implementation. • Identify potential crises with those affected; create crisis prevention or contingency plans for reducing or managing plans.	• Demonstrate success. • Provide resources and support. • Acknowledge efforts.	• Utilize crisis and contingency plans. • Allow for, listen to, and manage peoples' reactions (e.g., change isn't going to happen, poor planning or communication, insecurity, disillusionment, etc.). • Work closely with people to identify and resolve problems. • Turn crises into opportunities.	• Create and show visible success as soon as possible. • Provide resources and support.	• Allow people to work on their own resolve. • Monitor progress and provide appropriate ongoing support. • Acknowledge/reward success. • Utilize appropriate performance management techniques with die-hard resistors (e.g., coaching, consequence management, etc.).

Thoughts

I. Excitement	II. Acceleration	III. Crisis or opportunity	IV. Reacceleration	V. Continuation on resolve
"Let's give it a try."	"Maybe this will work."	"It's not going to happen." or "Let's give it one more shot."	"Maybe this will work after all."	"We did it!"

Source: Adapted by permission of Judith G. Noel, president, Seapoint Consulting Corporation, Kittery Point, ME 03905 (207) 439-6434.

Exercise 8.3

Consider the change project that you identified in Exercise 8.1. Given the anticipated patterns in any change process, identify how you would plan for the following phases.

Phase I: Excitement

_____

_____

_____

_____

_____

Phase II: Acceleration

_____

_____

_____

_____

_____

Phase III: Crisis or Opportunity

_____

_____

_____

_____

_____

Phase IV: Reacceleration and Increased Momentum

_____

_____

_____

_____

_____

Phase V: Continuation on Resolve

_____

_____

_____

_____

8

BARRIERS TO CHANGE IMPLEMENTATION

Successful change strategies must take into consideration any implementation barriers that presently exist or may arise during a change effort. Once these are identified, plans will need to be made to either resolve them or limit their negative effects. Here are some of the more common barriers and their consequences.*

Barriers to Implementation	Consequences
▪ Lack of corporate vision and strategy.	Inability of people to clearly interpret change efforts.
▪ Lack of organizational priorities and/or resources necessary to support them.	Wheel spinning activity; frustration; increased "quit and stay" mentality.
▪ Lack of effective change planning.	Failure to implement change effectively and with lasting results.
▪ Lack of clear communication and direction.	Messages are diffused, less specific, and open to arbitrary interpretation.
▪ Lack of understanding, belief, or support from those who must see the change carried out.	Ineffective sponsorship and follow through.
▪ Lack of preparation and planning for resistance.	Increased resistance, often moving from overt to covert (e.g., sabotage, work slowdowns, compliance without commitment).
▪ Lack of change success (e.g., history of poor or failed implementation).	Limited faith in or support for change initiatives.
▪ Lack of leadership credibility and/or trust.	Directives are ignored or not taken seriously.
▪ Lack of demonstrated support for risk taking (e.g., "Take all the risks you want, just don't make a mistake.").	Promotes environment for low risk taking; negatively impacts receptivity to change; limits personal and organizational growth.
▪ Lack of involvement, two-way communication, or synergy.	Missed opportunities for higher quality ideas, enhanced commitment, and decreased resistance.
▪ Lack of middle-management commitment and support.	Lack of enthusiasm and support necessary to carry the change forward.
▪ Lack of critical role identification, preparation, and accountability (e.g., initiating and sustaining sponsors, agents, targets, and advocates).	Mismanaged change resulting in no change (e.g., black hole syndrome), distorted change, or short-term change.
▪ Lack of consequence management (e.g., established structure or procedure for rewarding compliance and managing noncompliance).	Those affected by the change will learn to ignore directives.

*Source: Adapted from *How to Be an Effective Sponsor of Organizational Change*, p. 4, Copyright 1989, with permission of Daryl R. Conner, ODR, Inc., 2900 Chamblee–Tucker Rd., Atlanta, GA 30341.

Barriers to Implementation	Consequences
■ Lack of time to adjust to and implement change effectively.	Implementation of change will be unsupported or mismanaged, resulting in "rework" and/or morale damage.
■ Lack of effective role modeling and example setting (e.g., saying one thing but doing another).	Aborted or incomplete change; failure to achieve desired results.

BRIDGES FOR CHANGE IMPLEMENTATION

How can you play an active role in building bridges for successful change implementation? Here are some ideas:

- Educate people about change.

- Require change planning.

- Manage change as a process.

- Assess organizational readiness (e.g., corporate culture, timing, resources, etc.).

- Identify and utilize critical roles (e.g., initiating and sustaining sponsors, agents, targets, advocates).

- Demonstrate commitment through active involvement and role modeling.

- Promote synergy and teamwork.

- Anticipate resistance and plan for it.

- Objectively assess and prepare for implementation barriers.

- Demand that structure and discipline be applied to the planning and implementation of all change initiatives.

- Communicate clearly, regularly, and openly.

- Provide necessary resources and support.

- Limit crises. When and if they do come, turn them into opportunities.

- Follow through.

■ Exercise 8.4

Consider the change project that you identified in Exercise 8.1. Identify the barriers and bridges to its successful implementation.

Barriers	Bridges

Chapter 8 Checkpoints

✓ Costs of failure in managing change include unresolved problems or lost opportunities; wasted time, money, and human or material resources; morale decline; job insecurity; ignored future directives; loss of leadership credibility; and organizational well-being.

✓ Criteria for evaluating and measuring change success should include the stated goals and objectives of the change (human and technical), time frames for implementation, budget, and expected organizational benefits or added value.

✓ Patterns in the change process can be used to identify, effectively prepare for, and manage critical points in a change effort.

✓ Before beginning any change initiative, it is essential to anticipate and plan for implementation barriers as well as bridges.

9 | Understanding and Managing Resistance

This chapter will help you to:

- Understand where resistance comes from.
- Assess stakeholder dispositions.
- Identify why individuals may resist change.
- Identify why organizations may resist change.
- Develop ideas for preventing, reducing, and managing resistance.

Change from Above

Puradyne, a waste-energy treatment plant, had been serving companies for some 20 years. During the first 17 years it had grown and prospered, but in recent years it faced spiraling economic downturns. Not only was Puradyne's customer base declining as client companies went out of business, but among those that remained, less work was subcontracted out to it.

As time passed, it became apparent that for Puradyne to survive it would need to expand its customer base or change its service product, and perhaps do some of both. Senior managers met for months to discuss and develop a plan for resolving this problem. A plan finally did emerge, and the employees were brought together for a companywide briefing. The president addressed the group as follows:

"We have brought you all here today to inform you about some changes that will be affecting you at Puradyne. Next month we will be positioning ourselves to service the needs of new customers. This may entail extensive changes in our treatment processes and current work schedules. Your full cooperation with this effort is expected for the good of the company."

Employees left the auditorium disgruntled. Most did not know why the changes were necessary and what they would mean for them. Their imaginations went wild.

The following day, top-down change implementation began. Processes would be adjusted dramatically to adhere to the needs of a major new customer. Managers were met with major resistance behavior ranging from denial to outright sabotage. ■

■ Questions to Consider

1. What do you think led to the resistance?

_____

_____

_____

2. What reasons might people in this situation have for resisting?

_____

_____

_____

3. What steps would you take to prevent, reduce, or manage this resistance?

_____

_____

_____

WHERE DOES RESISTANCE TO CHANGE COME FROM?

In any change initiative, some level of resistance should be expected and planned for. Change brings the inevitability of conflict emerging from differences of opinion. In conflict there is both opportunity and danger. The opportunity is to enable people to become part of the change process, resulting in increased commitment and support. The danger is to leave the conflict unresolved, resulting in peoples' desire to erode or sabotage a process. If left unmanaged, what do you think Puradyne employees would do?

A key to managing resistance is to understand that its primary source is not usually the change itself but the disruption that it represents. This disruption is caused when a change does not fit easily into existing individual or organizational frames of reference and paradigms.

■ Exercise 9.1

Consider a change that you wish to make in your workplace. Identify anticipated disruptions that your change may cause.

_____

_____

_____

_____

_____

ASSESSING STAKEHOLDER DISPOSITIONS

Identifying stakeholders and their anticipated dispositions regarding a change is crucial to managing resistance. Stakeholders are people who are affected directly or indirectly by a change. The effect can be positive, negative, or even neutral. Stakeholders may include employees, suppliers, customers, and anyone else who is affected by a change.

Once your stakeholders are identified, it is imperative to anticipate their disposition regarding the change. You will find that there will be individual differences, just as there are individual frames of reference and paradigms. As you identify where your resistance will be coming from, you can develop plans to manage it. You may even discover welcome sources of individual support, which can help positively influence others and orchestrate your change.

■ Exercise 9.2

Consider a specific change that you would like to make in your workplace and complete the following stakeholder assessment form.

STAKEHOLDER ASSESSMENT FORM

List all of your stakeholders. Place an N in the corresponding column to indicate where the stakeholders are now. Place an ∗ in the corresponding column to indicate where they need to be in order for your change to be implemented.

Individual Names/Department (if applicable)	Block	Allow	Help	Make

Terms:

Block (person will actively work against the change).

Allow (person will let the change happen).

Help (person will actively support the change).

Make (person will actually implement or carry out the change—for example, receptive targets).

Source: Adapted by permission of Judith G. Noel, president, Seapoint Consulting Corporation, Kittery Point, ME 03095, (207) 439-6434

By completing the stakeholder assessment form, you have identified individuals who need attention. Questions such as Whom should I start with? or How much support is really needed to effect change? will arise, and you can begin to address them.

In any change effort, people generally fall into one of three categories, or reaction zones: comfort, risk, or panic. These are shown graphically on page 93.

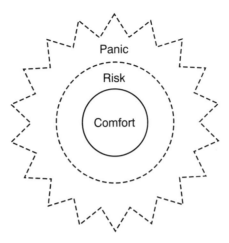

A natural tendency is to focus first on individuals who show the greatest level of resistance—those in the panic zone. This, in fact, may not be the best use of your time, energy, and resources.

An inside-out approach will be less time consuming and far more effective. Those in the comfort zone can serve to build your base of support and positively influence those in the risk zone. As your base of support builds, those who were once in the risk zone can positively influence those in the panic zone. Utilizing others as supporters can not only lessen acceptance time but strengthen overall support for your change. Other peoples' influence by virtue of relationship, whether peer or otherwise, may be met with greater receptivity than your own.

It is not necessary to have everyone carrying the flag at the same time for change implementation. It is critical, however, that all stakeholders at least move to the allow box, or risk-taking zone. To the extent that greater support is needed to carry out a change, a plan must be developed to work with each individual.

WHY DO INDIVIDUALS RESIST CHANGE?

In Exercise 9.2 you may have identified stakeholders whom you expect to block your change. A useful follow-up question is Why might each of these individuals want to block this change? or What might be causing the disruption in their frame of reference or paradigms? In the answers lies the key to managing individual resistance. Sources of individual resistance usually fall into one or more of the following categories: values, emotions, knowledge, and behaviors. People often perceive that change will result in a number of negative consequences, including the following:

- Loss of control (real or perceived).
- Uncertainty.
- Disruption of habits and routines.
- Increased workload.
- Inability to do the new job.
- Not enough time to adjust.
- Not enough resources for implementation.

People also resist change because they may not agree with a change or the reason for a particular change is not clear to them. This resistance may occur for a number of reasons:

- Lack of information.
- Inadequate resources devoted to implementation.
- The source of the change has limited credibility.
- Lack of faith or trust in the leadership.
- The change doesn't seem right for the organization.

WHY DO ORGANIZATIONS RESIST CHANGE?

Sources of organizational resistance can include logistics, economics, and politics. Here are a few illustrations:

- "It doesn't feel right."
- "The timing is 'wrong.' We have too many other things on our plate right now."
- "We can't afford to do it."
- "X wouldn't go for it."
- "We don't have the resources to accomplish it."

Exercise 9.3

Refer back to your stakeholder assessment from Exercise 9.2. List each "blocker" below and indicate the specific reasons you think they may resist. Next, identify possible solutions for each.

Individuals	Reasons for Resistance	Possible Solutions
_____	_____	_____
_____	_____	_____
_____	_____	_____
_____	_____	_____
_____	_____	_____
_____	_____	_____
_____	_____	_____
_____	_____	_____

WHAT ARE SOME WAYS TO PREVENT, REDUCE, AND MANAGE RESISTANCE?

One of the best ways to manage resistance is to prevent or substantially reduce it. In earlier chapters, you were introduced to many techniques for accomplishing this. They are summarized below.

- **Involvement.** Involve people in change decisions and implementation plans as much and as early on as possible. People are much less likely to resist their own ideas.

- **Communication.** Communicate clearly and frequently. Allow for two-way dialogue to achieve understanding and acceptance.

- **Gradual implementation.** Break change implementation into manageable, visible, and achievable steps.

- **Commitment.** Demonstrate your own commitment and allow commitment from others to develop naturally.

- **Leadership.** Demonstrate skill in effective change planning and implementation.

- **Empowerment.** Empower people as part of the process.

- **Reward.** Reward progress rather than perfection alone. Use rewards that are meaningful to the receivers. Celebrate success.

- **Resources.** Provide resources and support necessary for people to achieve a change.

- **Utilize and acknowledge supporters.** Use these people as positive examples or role models to move the change effort forward. Establish critical roles and responsibilities.

- **Avoid the we/they syndrome.** Celebrate the past and build excitement for the future.

- **Promote risk taking.** Establish trust by starting with low-risk projects or parts of larger projects that are short term and likely to be successful.

At times you will encounter some very specific reasons why people may resist change. These may require specific, rather than general, solutions for each individual.

9

Chapter 9 Checkpoints

✓ The primary source of resistance is not the change itself but the perceived or real disruption it represents.

✓ Stakeholders may have a variety of reactions to change (e.g., block, allow, help, make), which can be assessed and managed effectively.

✓ Individuals resist change for a variety of reasons, usually based on values, emotions, knowledge, and behaviors.

✓ Organizations resist change for a variety of reasons, usually based on logistics, economics, and politics.

✓ Resistance can be prevented, reduced, and managed by utilizing effective change planning and implementation techniques, while allowing for individual differences.

CHAPTER

10 | Communicating Change Effectively

┌───┐

This chapter will help you to:

- Identify the steps of change.
- Learn how the steps of change relate to change commitment.
- Integrate change principles into an effective communication process.

└───┘

Downsizing Difficulties

Changes for Us, a large clothing retail store, had been in business for some 50 years. Not unlike many other retailers, business had dropped substantially over the past year due to the economy. To survive, the company determined that it would need to achieve a 20 percent reduction in force over the next six months. Department heads were charged with informing their employees about this change.

As the head of the computer department met with one of his employees, the following conversation transpired:

Manager:
"We've been told that we need to achieve a 20 percent reduction in force over the next six months."

Employee:
"But you told me this job was secure when I came to work for you five years ago!"

Manager:
"Well that was then and this is now."

Employee:
"So, am I going to be laid off?"

Manager:
"I don't like your attitude, young man. Keep it up and you can bet on it."

Employee:

"Well, spare yourself the aggravation. I've had enough. I quit!"

The employee packed up his belongings and left. The manager sat shaking his head. He had been planning to tell this employee that because of vacancies in his department, he didn't think anyone would be laid off. Instead, people would be cross-trained and have to assume a little more responsibility. Now he was losing one of his top performers, and he wondered what went wrong. ■

■ Questions to Consider

1. What went wrong with this change process?

_____

_____

_____

2. What questions and concerns did the employee have that were not addressed?

_____

_____

_____

3. What suggestions would you make for improving this change communication?

_____

_____

_____

Effective communication is indeed the bridge between strategic plans for change and their realization. Far too often the importance of communication is overlooked, and for this reason great change plans never come to fruition.

THE STEPS OF CHANGE

As you discovered in Chapter 6, there is no such thing as a straight-line approach to managing change. Instead, you must acknowledge that the essence of change management is managing people through transitions. People generally do not take one giant step from becoming aware of a problem to achieving immediate success. Instead, they go through incremental stages of awareness, understanding, acceptance, and finally the change itself. The seven steps of change are:

1. Describe the change.
2. Explain the impact of the change.
3. Encourage questions and allow for concerns.
4. Respond to questions and concerns.
5. Restate alternative behaviors.
6. Gain commitment.
7. Confirm plans and create a follow-through process.

Considering Individual Background Information

As you prepare for communicating any change, you must consider the receivers. Who are they? What is their background in the company? and How might they respond to the change? While you should always check your assumptions throughout the communication process, considering questions such as these will provide you with a place to begin your communication planning.

■ Exercise 10.1

Consider a change situation that you will need to communicate to an employee. Begin your preparation by answering the following questions:

1. What is the current work environment (e.g., office, computer room, manufacturing floor, etc.)?
2. What is the employee's present job?
3. What is the employee's work history?
4. Describe the change situation. (Be sure to consider the impact on the employee.)
5. What is the anticipated employee behavior toward the change (i.e., feelings/reactions, levels of resistance, reasons for resistance, etc.)?
6. What is the expected employee response?

10

AN EFFECTIVE COMMUNICATION PROCESS

It is necessary to have a process for communicating change that takes each step (awareness, understanding, acceptance, and change) into account. The following process does just this:

1. **Describe the change and the reasons for it.** This step increases the employee's general awareness.

2. **Explain the impact the change will have on the employee.** This step adds to the employee's personal awareness regarding the change by providing an opportunity to clarify and express feelings.

3. **Encourage questions and allow for the expression of concerns.** This step adds to the employee's understanding of the change by providing an opportunity to clarify and express feelings.

4. **Respond to any questions and concerns.** This step leads to initial acceptance.

5. **Restate or re-emphasize alternative behaviors and methods.** This step clarifies expectations.

6. **Gain commitment to the change.** This step ensures that the employee has a commitment to adopt and implement the change effectively.

7. **Confirm implementation plans and establish follow-through procedures.** This step further clarifies expectations, progress measurements, and ongoing support necessary for change success.

The following is an example of how this process might unfold.

---

1. Describe the change and the reasons for it.

Manager: "As you are aware, the company will be downsizing the computer department over the next six months."

2. Explain the impact the change will have on the individual affected.

Manager: "This will be accomplished by placing a hiring freeze on our current openings and through natural attrition. People currently employed who wish to remain in their positions, including you, will have an opportunity to do so. The change will affect you and others in the department in workload only. I will be asking you to train for and assume additional responsibilities in order to fill the gap. A training schedule will be established early next week, once assignments are finalized. Unfortunately, the company cannot offer you additional money at this time due to financial constraints."

3. Encourage questions and allow for the expression of concerns.	Employee: "You've got to be kidding. There isn't enough time to get our work done now. How can the company expect us to keep taking on more? How will we even make the time for training? Will they cut the other departments like this too?"
4. Respond to any questions and concerns. (If no questions or concerns are raised by the receiver, the sender should encourage them through open-ended questioning.)	Manager: "I realize that you have a full workload and are concerned about being able to continue doing a good job if you have to take on additional responsibilities. I have asked that our large research project deadline be extended to allow us to train for and begin implementing these changes. The company has agreed to extend our deadline by one month. Other departments are also being asked to cut by 20 percent. Unfortunately, this is necessary in order to stabilize our financial condition. All of us will have to work smarter and a little harder across the board. To support you in this process, I'm willing to work with you to see if we can streamline some of our procedures."
5. Restate or re-emphasize alternative behaviors and methods.	Manager: "As I've mentioned, we'll all need to take on a little more of a workload in order to fill the gap. Training and time to train will be provided for, and as much as possible we will look to see where we can streamline."
6. Gain commitment to the change.	Manager: "May I have your commitment to give it a try?" (If yes, acknowledge the employee and go to 7. If no, ask why and respond to further questions and concerns until commitment is achieved. Where appropriate and necessary, utilize consequence management.)
7. Confirm implementation plans and establish follow-through procedures.	Manager: "I'll be discussing the training schedule with you on Tuesday of next week. Training will start on the following Monday and continue for a week. Following the training I would like to meet with you to hear your suggestions for how we might streamline our operations [establish a date]. I'll be checking back with you during our weekly meetings as to how things are going. Please feel free to come to me with any problems, concerns, or suggestions in the meantime."

10

■ Exercise 10.2

Consider the planning that you completed in Exercise 10.1. Develop an outline, using the change communication process just discussed.

1. Describe the change and the reasons for it.

2. Explain the impact the change will have on the employee.

3. Encourage questions and allow for the expression of concerns.

4. Respond to any questions and concerns.

5. Restate or reemphasize alternative behaviors and methods.

6. Gain commitment to the change.

7. Confirm implementation plans and establish follow-through procedures.

A good way to check and improve upon your plan is to role-play. Explain or give your change communication planning to a partner and ask him or her to play the role of your employee. Encourage your partner to respond realistically and to challenge you as you play the role of the manager or yourself.

Before starting your role-play, take a minute to review these important communication guidelines:

- Remember to always maintain employee self-esteem.
- Be sure to focus on behavior, not personality.
- Encourage employee involvement and participation.
- Listen carefully to hear employee questions and concerns and respond to them.
- Communicate clearly and concisely.
- Observe, probe, and respond to nonverbal signals.

Following your role-play, evaluate your own performance and get feedback from your "employee" partner, using the critique form on the following page.

10

CHANGE COMMUNICATION CRITIQUE FORM

Record your comments in the spaces below as you observe how the manager applied the communication process and each of the communication guidelines described earlier.

Communication Process Steps

1. Describe the change and the reasons for it.

_____

_____

_____

_____

_____

2. Explain the impact the change will have on the employee.

_____

_____

_____

_____

_____

3. Encourage questions and allow for the expression of concerns.

_____

_____

_____

_____

_____

4. Respond to any questions and concerns.

_____

_____

_____

_____

_____

5. Restate or reemphasize alternative behaviors and methods.

_____

_____

_____

_____

_____

(continued)

10

CHANGE COMMUNICATION CRITIQUE FORM
(concluded)

Communication Process Steps

6. Gain commitment to the change.

_____

_____

_____

_____

_____

7. Confirm implementation plans and establish follow-through procedures.

_____

_____

_____

_____

_____

_____

Communication Guidelines

Rate demonstrated use of the following from 1 to 3, with 3 being the highest rating.

_____   Employee self-esteem was maintained.

_____   Discussion stayed focused on behavior, not personality.

_____   Employee involvement and participation were encouraged.

_____   Employee was listened to.

_____   Messages were clear and concise.

_____   Nonverbal signals were picked up and responded to.

Ideas for Improvement

_____

_____

_____

_____

_____

Chapter 10 Checkpoints

✓ The steps of change are awareness, understanding, acceptance, and change.

✓ The steps of change have a direct correlation to change commitment. As each step along the way is handled well, the level of change commitment generally increases.

✓ An effective change communication process requires consideration of the individual and utilization of the following seven-step process:
1. Describe the change and the reasons for it.
2. Explain the impact the change will have on the employee.
3. Encourage questions and allow for the expression of concerns.
4. Respond to any questions and concerns.
5. Restate or reemphasize alternative behaviors.
6. Gain commitment to the change.
7. Confirm implementation plans and establish a follow-through process.

✓ Communication should be planned ahead of time yet allow for flexibility at the time of delivery.

THE END OF ONE JOURNEY AND THE START OF ANOTHER

Congratulations! You have now completed your journey through *Managing Change in the Workplace*. Along the way you have been introduced to and developed many new skills. Effective change management, however, is a long journey and in many respects we have just begun.

Each change we face presents new circumstances, challenges, and opportunities. As change leaders we have not only the responsibility, but the privilege of encouraging and guiding others through change journeys. As we all learn to initiate and embrace change, we will do much to forward our organizations and the people within them.

Post-Test

Respond to the following statements to test your understanding of the key ideas in this book. Circle the letter that best completes the statement. If you have difficulty with any of the questions, refer back to the text to review the key concepts.

1. Organizations would be better off if they:
    a. Always stayed the same.
    b. Worked to continually improve.
    c. Changed occasionally when forced to.

2. Managing change begins:
    a. Within yourself.
    b. With people who have to carry out the change.
    c. With people who make change decisions.

3. When new ideas do not fit existing organizational rules and regulations, they should be:
    a. Screened out.
    b. Altered until they do.
    c. Still heard and considered.

4. When an organizational change is announced, the first thing people want to know is how it will affect:
    a. The organizational culture.
    b. Organizational politics and management.
    c. Themselves.

5. The most difficult type of change to manage usually is:
    a. Transitional.
    b. Transformational.
    c. Developmental.

6. Change should be managed:

    a. Quickly and directly with a straight-line approach.

    b. Gradually as a process.

    c. Indirectly, so people won't realize it is happening.

7. Critical roles in the change process are:

    a. Initiating and sustaining sponsors.

    b. Advocates.

    c. Targets.

8. The most significant cost in failing to manage a needed change well is that:

    a. The change is distorted.

    b. No change occurs.

    c. Organizational opportunity and potential go unrealized.

9. Individual resistance to change is caused primarily by the:

    a. Change itself.

    b. Fact that people just do not like change.

    c. Disruption to people's frames of reference.

10. Change communication can be effectively planned for by considering the following sequential steps toward change commitment:

    a. Awareness, understanding, acceptance, and change.

    b. Change, awareness, understanding, and acceptance.

    c. Understanding, awareness, change, and acceptance.

SOLUTIONS

1. b   2. a   3. c   4. c   5. b

6. b   7. c   8. c   9. c   10. a

Business Skills Express Series

This growing series of books addresses a broad range of key business skills and topics to meet the needs of employees, human resource departments, and training consultants.

To obtain information about these and other Business Skills Express books, please call Irwin Professional Publishing toll free at: 1-800-634-3966.

Effective Performance Management
ISBN   1-55623-867-3

Hiring the Best
ISBN   1-55623-865-7

Writing that Works
ISBN   1-55623-856-8

Customer Service Excellence
ISBN   1-55623-969-6

Writing for Business Results
ISBN   1-55623-854-1

Powerful Presentation Skills
ISBN   1-55623-870-3

Meetings That Work
ISBN   1-55623-866-5

Effective Teamwork
ISBN   1-55623-880-0

Time Management
ISBN   1-55623-888-6

Assertiveness Skills
ISBN   1-55623-857-6

Motivation at Work
ISBN   1-55623-868-1

Overcoming Anxiety at Work
ISBN   1-55623-869-X

Positive Politics at Work
ISBN   1-55623-879-7

Telephone Skills at Work
ISBN   1-55623-858-4

Managing Conflict at Work
ISBN   1-55623-890-8

The New Supervisor: Skills for Success
ISBN   1-55623-762-6

The *Americans with Disabilities Act:* What Supervisors Need to Know
ISBN   1-55623-889-4

Managing the Demands of Work and Home
ISBN   0-7863-0221-6

Effective Listening Skills
ISBN   0-7863-0102-4

Goal Management at Work
ISBN   0-7863-0225-9

Positive Attitudes at Work
ISBN   0-7863-0100-8

Supervising the Difficult Employee
ISBN   0-7863-0219-4

Cultural Diversity in the Workplace
ISBN   0-7863-0125-2

Managing Change in the Workplace
ISBN   0-7863-0162-7

Negotiating for Business Results
ISBN   0-7863-0114-7

Practical Business Communication
ISBN   0-7863-0227-5

High Performance Speaking
ISBN   0-7863-0222-4

Delegation Skills
ISBN   0-7863-0105-9

Coaching Skills: A Guide for Supervisors
ISBN   0-7863-0220-8

Customer Service and the Telephone
ISBN   0-7863-0224-0

Creativity at Work
ISBN   0-7863-0223-2

Effective Interpersonal Relationships
ISBN   0-7863-0255-0

The Participative Leader
ISBN   0-7863-0252-6

Building Customer Loyalty
ISBN   0-7863-0253-4

Getting and Staying Organized
ISBN   0-7863-0254-2

Total Quality Selling
ISBN   0-7863-0324-7

Business Etiquette
ISBN   0-7863-0323-9

Empowering Employees
ISBN   0-7863-0309-3

Training Skills for Supervisors
ISBN   0-7863-0308-5